P9-CDW-068

Of MIKES *and* MEN

A Lifetime of
Braves Baseball

Pete Van Wieren with Jack Wilkinson

TRIUMPH
BOOKS

Copyright © 2010 by Pete Van Wieren and Jack Wilkinson

No part of this publication may be reproduced, stored in a retrieval system, or transmitted in any form by any means, electronic, mechanical, photocopying, or otherwise, without the prior written permission of the publisher, Triumph Books, 542 South Dearborn Street, Suite 750, Chicago, Illinois 60605.

Triumph Books and colophon are registered trademarks of Random House, Inc.

Library of Congress Cataloging-in-Publication Data

Van Wieren, Pete.
 Of mikes and men : a lifetime of Braves baseball / Pete Van Wieren
with Jack Wilkinson.
     p. cm.
 Includes index.
 ISBN 978-1-60078-359-3
 1. Van Wieren, Pete . 2. Sportscasters—United States—Biography. 3. Atlanta
Braves (Baseball team)—History. I. Wilkinson, Jack, 1950– II. Title.
 GV742.42.V36A3 2010
 796.092—dc22
 [B]
                              2010003483

This book is available in quantity at special discounts for your group or organization. For further information, contact:
 Triumph Books
 542 South Dearborn Street
 Suite 750
 Chicago, Illinois 60605
 (312) 939–3330
 Fax (312) 663–3557
 www.triumphbooks.com

Printed in U.S.A.
ISBN: 978-1-60078-359-3
Design by Patricia Frey
All photos courtesy of the author unless otherwise indicated.

For my mother and Elaine, who shared it all

Contents

Chapter 1

The Long Drive Home

I n the early afternoon of October 21, 2008, the drive from my home in Alpharetta, Georgia, to Turner Field seemed no different than the one I had made hundreds, no, thousands of times before. I really didn't feel any different that day. But the purpose of that drive was very different, indeed.

On that day, I was announcing my retirement after 33 years as an Atlanta Braves broadcaster and after 43 years in the sports broadcasting business.

It's 30 miles from our home down to the ballpark. The drive took about an hour. You've got the usual battle with Atlanta traffic. Driving in, you're just thinking about getting there. That Tuesday, I wasn't thinking about anything except getting to the ballpark.

I turned into the media parking lot at Turner Field and pulled into my regular parking space, number 15. I walked across Bill Lucas Drive, up the steps to the media entrance, past the security checkpoint, then I proceeded down the tunnel past the Braves clubhouse and turned right down the hallway to the press conference room.

I peeked into the room, and that's when it really struck me.

The broadcasters were there, along with our longtime TV producer, Glenn Diamond. John Schuerholz, the Braves president, was there. General manager Frank Wren and several other members of the Braves' front office, too. And when I saw all the media, that's when it really hit home that I was about to embark on a major lifestyle change. Normally, when I'd go into that room, I would be sitting with them; joining all my colleagues from the media and hearing the manager or general manager announce the news of a trade or a player getting a contract extension.

But this time, it would be me up on that platform. When I saw everyone there, I thought, "Whoops! I guess this is gonna be a little different."

The news of my retirement, which broke first that morning on radio and then on the Internet, caught nearly everyone by surprise. And as I'd neared the ballpark, I kept reminding myself to make it clear why this decision was made. It was not a spur-of-the-moment thing. It was something my family and I had talked about for a year. Something I had decided as far back as the All-Star break.

It had been a horrible year. But I wasn't retiring because of the untimely death of my friend and longtime broadcast partner, Skip Caray, who died of heart failure in early August. I was not stepping down because the team had fallen to its first 90-loss season since 1990. Yes, the team played terribly and was down 17, 18 games at the All-Star break. But that wasn't the reason I was retiring. And I wasn't leaving because of any health issues.

The decision process actually began just before spring training that season, when I met with Braves vice president Derek Schiller. "Your contract is up at the end of the year," he reminded me. "So we need to talk at some point about a new one. You're here as long as you want to be, so give it some thought and we'll get together during the season."

While I appreciated the generosity of the offer, I knew then that I might not accept it. I still had a great passion for the game. I worked for an outstanding organization. In short, I loved my job. Why then did I decide to leave?

The answer, very simply, is the schedule. The daily schedule. I wanted to have some years where it didn't rule my life. Many interpreted that as the travel schedule, but that's not what I meant. Major League Baseball travel is easy: charter flights, equipment managers to handle the luggage, hotel keys waiting when you arrive. There was nothing stressful about that. The schedule I'm referring to is the daily effort required to do the best possible job for the fans—who are the lifeblood of the game.

When I was hired by the Braves in December 1975 by Ernie Johnson, he and his wife, Lois, gave my wife, Elaine, and I a plaque that said, "We interrupt this marriage to bring you the baseball season." You can't help but smile when you read that, but there's a strong element of truth in that statement.

Elaine always called it my "baseball mode." She'd say, "From the time of the 400 Club (a Braves fan club) banquet each January to the end of the season, you were locked in—24/7."

Indeed, any success I had as a broadcaster came because of my preparation for each and every game.

A typical day for me began like this: as soon as I got up, I started with a check of the newspapers in whatever city we were in. At home, we had the *Atlanta Journal-Constitution, USA Today*, and the *New York Times* delivered. On the road, I'd go down to the hotel newsstand and pick up whatever papers were available, sometimes as many as a half-dozen in New York and several in Chicago.

Once the Internet arrived, many of those papers were online and the list of information sources expanded exponentially. That process usually lasted at least an hour, often longer. When I was up to speed on all that had happened in baseball the day before, it was time to begin prepping for the upcoming game.

First, I would put together my Diamond Notes pregame radio show. This was a three-minute feature that became very popular with listeners—a combination of facts, figures, history, trivia, and information on all facets of the game. Next, I'd begin working on the notes for the game itself. I always looked for some perspective to better portray what was happening on the field.

For example, in 2005, Jeff Francoeur burst onto the Braves' scene with five home runs in his first 12 games. To give this fact some meaning, I went back and researched how many games it took for some of the Braves' leading home-run hitters to hit their first five homers. The results:

- Andruw Jones—15 games
- Bob Horner—26 games
- Chipper Jones—28 games
- Hank Aaron—32 games
- Dale Murphy—83 games

In fact, the only Brave who hit his first five home runs in a shorter span was an obscure third baseman, Jose Oliva, who hit five in his first 11 games in 1994. This information took about 30 seconds to report on the air but required about two hours of research plus a phone call to the Elias Sports Bureau to develop.

I always got to the ballpark early and was almost always the first member of the media to arrive. For a night game, I would usually be there by about 2:30 PM. My first stop would always be the Braves clubhouse, where I would check in with the manager, coaches, and any early-arriving players. I'd always talk to Bobby Cox and some coaches and players. Often, their comments one-on-one were much more candid than what the rest of the media would hear later.

For a 7:00 PM game, I'd get up to the broadcast booth by 3:00 PM. Usually there would be no one in the booth by then. Not even the producer. I'd often have a half-hour to myself to get things organized, to write down the lineups and organize notes for that night's game. I never wanted to get caught by surprise. That was my study hour. If there was a new player called up or traded for, I'd study up on him.

Shortly after Ernie hired me, he began calling me "The Professor." It initially had to do with my appearance, my glasses, but also with the way I went about doing my job. After awhile, I always felt a real obligation to live up to that nickname, that reputation. That all played a part in my daily work schedule.

After finishing in the broadcast booth, the pregame routine would vary on a daily basis. Some days you might have a manager's pregame show to do or other pregame interviews to record. Some days, there was a guest appearance—by phone—on one of our radio network affiliates; we had about 180 stations on the Braves network.

Occasionally, you would visit a group of sponsors in one of the team suites. Or you might spend 30 or 45 minutes signing autographs out on the fan plaza, once "Skip & Pete's Hall of Fame Barbecue" opened out there.

Skip and I alternated barbecue duty daily.

That schedule never varied.

Then came the game: at times a postgame interview or scoreboard show, and then back home or to the hotel to wind down and watch highlights from other games. And start all over again the next morning. This was the basic routine every day—then, like the instructions on a shampoo bottle, "Lather, rinse, repeat," each day from the beginning of March to possibly the end of October.

This was the schedule I was talking about. This was the schedule I had followed for more than 6,000 games in 78 major- and minor-league ballparks, and for some 1,000 other events in close to 100 stadiums and arenas all over the world.

For 33 years, the Atlanta Braves had given me the opportunity to live out my childhood dreams. To the regular-season work, add 128 postseason games. At the time of my retirement, only Vin Scully of the Dodgers—with 136—had called more postseason games for the same team in the history of the game.

But when I stepped into the room that day for the press conference, it felt very different up on that platform. As I looked out at all of the media—Joe Simpson was there and Lemmer, Mark Lemke—well, it hits you: You're going to miss being around those people. The camaraderie of the co-workers; your fellow broadcasters, writers, people you had dinner with every night—I'd never thought about that. I knew then that there were some elements of the game that I would really miss, and these comrades from the media were near the top of the list.

I had wanted to retire right when the season was over. But John Schuerholz said, "Take a few weeks off and see if you might want to change your mind." I followed that suggestion, but nothing changed.

Derek had told John and CEO Terry McGuirk. They were the only people—outside of my family—who knew. John told me, "You don't have to explain to me. My wife, Karen, and I have this talk every week."

That morning, once the news leaked out on radio, Terry McGuirk called me and said, "If you ever reconsider, if you want to come back, you're always welcome." At the press conference, John had some very nice things to say about me. "He's a guy who knew the game, the inside of the game, loved being inside the game, understood the game, had a joy and spirit about it that was so real and so consistent. He's a real baseball man."

That meant a lot coming from John. Bobby wasn't there because he'd had knee replacement surgery, and he didn't know. Nobody knew until it leaked out that morning.

It was really funny. I didn't know how it was going to feel because it had been well thought out, and we'd talked about it. Once the decision was made, and I had my mind made up, I didn't have any qualms about it. The basic thing I was concerned about that day was I wanted to make it as clear as I could that the reason for my retirement was the schedule. And that I was young enough and healthy enough to do other things.

That day, I got calls from, well, let's just say job offers. At the press conference, I said jokingly, "If I knew I was going to get three job offers in an hour, I'd have done this ten years ago."

After the press conference, which started at 3:00 PM, there was a reception in the Sun Trust Club. It was mostly Braves employees. Don Sutton, who was about to return to the Braves as a broadcaster after two years in Washington, flew in for that. By the time it was over, it was about 5:00, and I had to do interviews for the local TV stations.

Once I finally got home, Elaine asked, "How'd it go?"

She talked about how all the TV stations had covered it. For me, the press coverage from newspapers and radio and TV and the blogs—it was just overwhelming. You don't think about what kind of impact you're going to have on people. You're doing your job and doing the best you can.

But the feedback, all the columns, made me feel good about what I did. What Mark Bradley wrote in the *Atlanta Journal-Constitution*, and Furman Bisher's column, it really made you feel good.

From Mark Bradley's column of October 22, 2008:

"Pete wasn't the guy who told the jokes, but he was the guy who made the jokes resonate. He was the straight man to Skip Caray's smart aleck, the balance in the last great booth of an era now officially at its end.

"Those were the Braves of good ol' Ernie and funny ol' Skip and the learned Professor, and that was, in the grand scheme of things, as good as broadcasting ever got…. We who sat and listened will miss him every bit as much as we've missed Skip, maybe even more. See, Pete's was always the harder part.

"He had to do the homework and make sense of everything. He had to tell us how many outs there were when Skip was cracking jokes about alimony. Pete had to be the professional, and that's the only real way to remember him.

"Pete the pro's pro. Pete the Professor. Pete Van Wieren—another great Atlanta voice gone but not forgotten. Never ever forgotten."

From Furman Bisher's *Atlanta Journal-Constitution* column of October 25, 2008:

"I've said this several times before—never admitted it to Pete—that he has the perfect voice for baseball. He makes me feel that I'm right there beside him and he's talking right in my ear. It's a gentle voice. No whooping and yowling. It comes oozing through the speaker like honey out of a horn—and if that has the sound of patronization, I apologize. But it's true. There's nobody smoother than Pete delivering the game from his seat to yours. But not any longer.

"That's the depressing part of it. Pete has retired…There may be some as good down the line, but none better, and none whose style rests better on my ears. It's an honor to do him honor, such as it is."

You kind of feel like a third person, though, like you're not reading about yourself when you read all this. It's very humbling—just like it was in 2003, when Time Warner took Skip and me off TV and how the fans reacted. That's something a lot of people in other lines of work don't get to experience. You can be a great doctor and your patients love you, but you can't go online or read the paper to see that.

All the time, you hope you're doing the job they expect of you—especially the fans, the most important people out there. When you see that they do, it makes it all worthwhile—the flights, checking into hotels at 3:00 AM, the rain delays. And it was very gratifying to hear the comments from Bobby and the players. The one comment Bobby had made me feel very good: "Unlike a lot of other broadcasters, Pete was able to see the game from a manager's standpoint."

I think a lot of that came from all those cups of coffee with Bobby in all those hotel lobbies in the morning on the road.

When Chipper Jones and Tom Glavine came out and said they never heard any player complaints about my work, and if I had anything critical to say that I said it in the right way, well, that meant a lot.

Over the next few days, I got calls daily from other broadcasters. Joe Castiglione from Boston called. The Phillies guys called, Tom McCarthy. Dave Van Horne called from the Marlins. John Sterling, who worked with us doing Braves games for TBS, called from the Yankees.

There were emails from the Washington Nationals, and a great email from Duane Kuiper and Mike Krukow of the Giants. Then came the hundreds of cards, some from the likes of Ernie Harwell, Phil Niekro, and Tigers general manager Dave Dombrowski. But most of them came from fans I had never met but who felt like they knew me. All of that was very gratifying, to know they were thinking of me.

When I was driving home, I thought, "What a great ride it's been."

Just to do more than I ever thought I'd do. Driving home, it had all gone so well, but the thought occurred to me that I was going to miss the broadcasters from the other teams, too. I'd miss talking to Harry Kalas and the rest of the Phillies crew. To Vin Scully. To Pat Hughes and Ron Santo of the Cubs. And to Dave Van Horne, just to name a few.

And then I realized that I'd been lucky enough to work beside those guys for 33 years. You look in the booth next door and…wow! I had a chance to literally work beside them. Those were my heroes growing up: Jack Buck, Mel Allen, Red Barber, Vin Scully. That was a very special thing to be able to do.

Some people asked me that if I retired, would I get bored? I never really felt that I'd have any trouble with keeping busy. If I thought I'd be bored, or stir crazy, I'd never have retired. We'd talked about this a lot, after 43 years of broadcasting, and I had no fear that I was going to be bored.

Elaine and I left about two days later for Europe on a cruise—and eventually, our luggage caught up with us! I'm very pleased that more than a year has gone by now and I have plenty to do. And I have things to do with my grandkids who live right nearby us. I miss the game and I miss the people, but I don't miss the schedule. And I don't think I ever will.

It was a wonderful career, far more than I ever thought I would accomplish. Not only 33 years as a major league broadcaster, but most of it spent broadcasting to a national audience. Fifteen postseasons, including an unprecedented 14 in a row. Five World Series, beginning with the unforgettable "Worst-to-First" World Series of 1991. And, of course, Atlanta's only world championship in '95—one of three World Series I think we could have, and should have, won.

But now it was time to take a step back, spend more time with the family. To travel, read, relax, and reflect on the fortunate life I have lived.

At the very top of what I thought I'd miss are the fans who supported me throughout my career. There is no possible way to thank them enough for that support. Yes, there would be much I would miss. Leaving the Braves was not easy. But then, getting there was even tougher.

Chapter **2**

Growing, Going...Gone

Our address was 55 Swansea Park in Greece, New York. Home was a gray-shingled, two-story house with three bedrooms and one bathroom on a residential street in a blue-collar area of Greece, a suburb of Rochester. It was a typical *Leave It to Beaver* neighborhood, except folks went to work carrying lunch boxes, not briefcases.

The house belonged to my grandparents, Wilbur and Eunice Jardine. Also living there were my aunt, Helen Jardine, my mother, Ruth, and me. My father had died in World War II.

Our extended family included numerous aunts, uncles, and lots of cousins. Family gatherings—of which there were many for birthdays and holidays— typically included about 20 people. Nearly all of them were huge baseball fans, mostly of the Rochester Red Wings, the St. Louis Cardinals Triple A affiliate in the International League.

The radio was always on when the Red Wings were playing. Local radio stations also carried the New York Yankees on a regular basis and occasionally New York Giants and Brooklyn Dodgers games. As far back as I can remember, baseball was a part of my life.

Sundays were when the family most often attended games in person.

Sundays were almost always double-headers. From a very early age, I was begging to go, but no one wanted a little boy tagging along for a long Sunday at the ballpark.

Finally, on August 13, 1950, I went to my first game. I was five, and it was a rare Sunday single game on the schedule.

The Rochester Red Wings hosted the Jersey City Giants. I went with my grandfather, grandmother, my mother, and my Aunt Helen. I was all decked out in my white flannel Rochester Red Wings uniform. And the game went 22 innings! At the time, it was the longest game in International League history.

What's more, both starting pitchers went the distance! Tom Poholsky for Rochester and Andy Tomasic for Jersey City each pitched scoreless ball after the second inning. It took five hours and 15 minutes before the Red Wings finally won 3–2 in the bottom of the 22nd.

I still have two distinct memories from that game. A Rochester player, outfielder Larry Ciaffone, broke his ankle sliding into second base and was carried off on a stretcher. That was the first time I ever saw anyone suffer a serious injury, and that image haunted me for a long time. I also remember that at some point, we moved from our seats along the third-base line in the sun up under the cover of the grandstand for the remainder of the game.

Of all the games you could attend, we picked that day for my first one. Twenty-two innings! It turned out to be a unique way to start out. And that game really got me hooked on the Red Wings.

I listened to all their games on the radio and attended games whenever I could. I kept a scrapbook—box scores and pictures—and replayed the games with complete play-by-play accounts in the driveway alongside my house.

I'm sure the neighbors who lived on Swansea Park became accustomed to—and were annoyed by—the sounds of a sponge-rubber ball thumping off the garage door, then my high-pitched voice carrying on like Mel Allen, the great Yankees broadcaster, "There's a long fly ball! And…"

I had devised a game where if I threw the ball and it came right back to me, it was an out. But the garage door had horizontal ridges about every 2 feet. If the ball hit the edge of one of those ridges, it would carom off to the left or right at an angle.

Three lilac trees formed a border between our driveway and the next-door neighbors. If the ball rolled past the first tree, it was a double. Past the second tree, a triple. Past all three trees, a home run. If it stopped short of the trees, it was a single. I had a similar setup off to the right of the driveway, depending on which part of our backyard garden the ball entered.

About this time, I also discovered *The Sporting News*. The new edition came out every Sunday, and I couldn't wait to go down to the Dewey Avenue Pharmacy to pick one up each week. I had somehow learned to read before I ever went to school and was reading *TSN* from cover to cover in the first grade. Everybody else in first grade was reading *Dick and Jane* and I was reading Dick Young.

In 1951, when I was seven, one of my Christmas gifts was the first-ever *Baseball Encyclopedia* by Hy Turkin and S.C. Thompson. I still have that book. Years later, I looked it up and discovered that in the National League in 1950, the No. 1 batting average for the season—going 1-for-2, .500—was by Ernie Johnson, then a young pitcher with the Boston Braves and later the man who hired me in Atlanta.

My ability to read and also do math actually got me into trouble at No. 42 School. I was extremely bored as a first grader and was constantly getting into mischief. My teacher and the principal decided to have me skip second grade. I went directly from first grade to third. That settled me down, but it also made me a year younger than all of my classmates—a situation that existed for the rest of my school years.

I was still able to breeze through my schoolwork easily, however, which allowed me more time for my first love: baseball. Besides the backyard game, I was always playing in pick-up games with neighborhood kids. It didn't matter where we played...sometimes at a playground, sometimes in the street. Always playing.

I became a Little Leaguer the first year I was eligible (age 9 in those days). When the weather was bad, I had numerous baseball board games to play. First, it was Cadaco *All-Star Baseball*, with the circular discs and spinner. Later, I played *APBA* and *Big League Manager*, more sophisticated baseball replay games with updated player card sets every year.

Of course, I also collected baseball cards. I had several full sets during the 1950s, but I have no idea where they are now.

My favorite cards were of players I saw play for the Red Wings on their way to the majors. Most of them played for the St. Louis Cardinals, Rochester's parent team: Ray Jablonski, Rip Repulski, Wally Moon, Larry Jackson, Bill Virdon, Jackie Brandt, Bob Gibson, Bob Miller, Tim McCarver, and Ray Sadecki.

I always wished that the Red Wings themselves were on baseball cards, but there were no minor league card sets back then. Some players, like Luke Easter and Cot Deal, had been on a card at some point; but some of my other favorites, like Tommy Burgess and Gary Blaylock, never were.

I played Little League, Pony League, and Babe Ruth League baseball, usually as a pitcher. I wasn't bad, but I wasn't great, either.

Playing professionally would have been a dream come true for me. But since that seemed unlikely, I began to become more and more attracted to the broadcast booth.

The first Red Wing broadcaster I really remember was Jack Buck, who was their radio voice in 1953, the year before he joined the St. Louis Cardinals. After Buck came Tom Decker, then Joe Cullinane. At Red Wing Stadium (later renamed Silver Stadium), I used to watch them wind their way up through the grandstand, climb the spiral steps up to the roof, then disappear until I could get just a glimpse of them once they entered the broadcast booth.

The more I watched them, the more I wanted to someday do what they did. When I was in eighth grade at Charlotte Junior-Senior High School, I got the chance to make my dream known.

Our English teacher, Mrs. Balcom, gave us a career-planning assignment. We were to pick a profession from a list she had drawn up, and then do a report on that occupation: duties, skills required, educational requirements, etc. If there was something you wanted to do that was not on the list, you were asked to see Mrs. Balcom for her approval.

I went to her desk and told her I wanted to be a baseball announcer. I might as well have told her I wanted to be the King of England.

"This is so far-fetched," she laughed. "I want you to be reasonable with your choice." She then looked at a master list on her desk, where she was record-ing everyone's choice. "Here," she said, "no one has chosen optician. Do your report on that."

"But I don't want to be an optician," I argued. "I want to be a baseball broadcaster."

Again, Mrs. Balcom laughed and, shaking her head, said, "We have to be realistic, Peter. I'll just put you down for optician."

So optician it was. And what did I learn from doing that report? I knew I didn't want to be an optician.

My high school guidance counselor, Mr. Julian, wasn't very supportive, either. When we had a meeting on colleges to which I might apply, I suggested Syracuse, which was known for its strong journalism school.

But Mr. Julian wanted me to attend a liberal arts college to get a broad education, and if I wanted to write or broadcast, I could work for the school newspaper or radio station.

Steered in that direction, I applied to three schools. I didn't get into Hamilton College but was accepted by both Cornell and Colgate.

Cornell was my first choice, but it was going to be a financial squeeze to be able to go there. My high school had an assembly for college-bound seniors concerning scholarship aid that might be available. One possibility that caught my ear involved being the child of a deceased war veteran. Scholarship aid was almost automatic if you qualified.

I picked up an application form, but I did not tell my family. I knew Cornell would be tough for them to afford. I wanted this scholarship aid to be a pleasant surprise for them. One piece of information I didn't have was the date and place of my father's death, nor did I know his rank at the time.

I asked our school librarian, Mrs. Cashman, where I might find that information. She referred me to the public library and a series of volumes that listed all of the WWII casualties alphabetically.

The very next day, after school, I took a bus downtown to the main branch and found the books Mrs. Cashman had mentioned. But there was no Howard Van Wieren listed. I even looked under the letter W—sometimes the Van is mistaken for a middle name. Still no luck. The next day, I was telling this to my cousin, Fred, when his mother, my Aunt Mary, overheard me and said, "Your father didn't die in the war. You need to ask your mother about that."

Her tone wasn't angry. It was more like, "Somebody needs to tell you the truth."

Aunt Mary must have told my mother what happened. A couple of days later, my mother said, "We need to go for a ride. I need to tell you something." She took me for a drive along the shore of Lake Ontario and told me the true story about my father. It was not a pleasant tale.

In the spring of 1944, just after learning he was about to become a father for the first time, Howard Van Wieren left for work at the Coca-Cola Bottling Plant in Rochester. His job was driving a delivery truck supplying Coca-Cola to grocers, restaurants, and bars, then collecting the payments for those deliveries. Early that evening, the telephone rang at our house.

It was someone from Coca-Cola calling. They were looking for Howard.

He hadn't returned with the truck. The police were notified and it wasn't long before they found the truck parked behind the train station downtown. Howard was gone, and so were the day's receipts. The police continued their search but were unable to find him.

That fall, a couple of weeks after I was born on October 7, another phone call came to the house. It was Howard, wanting to know if he was a father yet. And was it a boy or a girl? When my mother asked Howard where he was, all he said was, "Somewhere in Florida."

My father said he wanted to come home and face the music, but could the family send him some money? Well, the family was not about to do that. My grandfather got on the phone and said, "We're not sending you any money." But they did agree to buy him a bus ticket back to Rochester.

On the day of his scheduled arrival, my mother went down to the bus terminal and waited throughout the day. Bus after bus pulled into the terminal and discharged its passengers. For hours, she sat there and waited. Howard never arrived. He had cashed in the ticket they'd sent him and taken off. We never heard from him again.

My mother was very, very distraught. She'd been there all day long. She still had a newborn baby to take care of and a job to get back to. She was a legal secretary and didn't have a lot of spare time.

Years later, people always asked me, "Why didn't you ever ask about what happened to your father?" I was always told he had died in the war. That he was killed somewhere by somebody. That was the fact, and that was it. We had such a big family, and it just never came up. There was nobody from the Van Wieren side of the family. It was all the Jardine side, my mother's side.

It would be years later until, piece by piece, I found out the whole truth about my father.

Despite the cost, the opportunity to attend an Ivy League school was too enticing. In September 1961, I headed off to Cornell University in Ithaca, about 90 miles southeast of Rochester.

Like many college freshmen away from home for the first time, I felt an exhilarating sense of freedom now that I was away from my family—and I dove into college life full bore. I rarely missed a sporting event. I was a regular at the dormitory bull sessions. I learned which taverns you could get into without proof of age—I was only 16, and the minimum drinking age in New York at that time was 18. And I followed the suggestion of my guidance counselor and landed a spot on the sports staff of the *Cornell Daily Sun*.

The *Sun* published five days a week, Monday through Friday, and at first my duties were in the office, learning the newspaper business.

For much of my freshman year, I was helping with page layouts, writing headlines and photo captions, and editing wire copy. Occasionally, an outside newspaper would ask for help covering a story. Once I was asked to cover a regatta for the *Baltimore Sun* that featured the Navy crew along with three Ivy League schools. A couple of days later, I received in the mail a cut-sheet containing the article and a check for five dollars.

These "stringer" opportunities popped up often and were a good way to make a couple of dollars.

My first byline assignment for the *Sun* came on May 22, 1962. I was sent to cover a non-league baseball game between Cornell and the University of Scranton. As the game approached, I was sitting in the tiny press box at Hoy Field, talking with a man I'd just met. He was Harry Dorish, the old major league pitcher with the Red Sox and White Sox who was then a scout for the Milwaukee Braves.

Dorish was there to look at two Cornell players: second baseman Pat Pennucci, who later signed with the Detroit Tigers and played in their farm system for a season; and centerfielder Gary Wood, who opted for the National Football League as a career backup quarterback with the Washington Redskins and New York Giants.

I started taking notes, thinking this might be a good story for the student paper on these Big Red prospects. About five minutes before game time, a kid came into the press box and said, "I need help. My announcer's not here. Can anybody help out?"

He was an engineer for the student radio station, WVBR, and could someone come to the radio booth and stand by in case the announcer didn't arrive by game time? There were only three of us in the press box: the P.A. announcer, Dorish, and me.

Harry elbowed me and said, "Go ahead, give it a try. You might like it. It's easier than writing."

"Why?" I asked. Harry replied, "When the game is over, you still have to work when you're a writer. When you're broadcasting, once the game's over, you're done."

So I went over to the radio booth and wound up broadcasting the entire game. Turned out the regular announcer, whose name I never knew, was in an automobile accident. He wasn't hurt, but he never made it.

And that's how I got started. I did okay, and I liked it. When I got back to the newspaper to write my story, a couple of co-workers who'd heard the broadcast complimented me on my pinch-hit performance. One guy asked, "When did you start broadcasting?" I said, "When I was about six years old."

The broadcasting seed was planted thanks to Harry Dorish—a scout for the Braves, the team that eventually hired me in Atlanta.

I still felt that newspaper work was my eventual destination though.

Besides working for the *Sun*, I joined the staff of the IFC (Inter Fraternity Council) monthly newspaper, reporting on intramural sports.

I also joined a band.

I was rushing all the fraternities, and after pledging Alpha Phi Delta, I learned they were forming a band. But their drummer was going to veterinarian school, and when the class schedules came out, he realized he'd be too busy to play. They were looking for somebody, and I said, "I can play drums. I played all through high school." I'd played in both the marching and show bands, and I jumped at the chance.

Back then, all the regional bands had names like "Somebody and the Somethings." Bobby Comstock and the Counts. Wilmer and the Dukes. Dave and the Gladiators. We really didn't have a lead guy; all five of us had our roles, and we were trying to come up with a name. There was a hit movie out then called *The Hustler*, starring Paul Newman and Jackie Gleason. Somebody said, 'Why don't we use it for the band?' And we became The Hustlers and put the name on my bass drum.

Carmine Lanciani was on bass. Dave Karr played rhythm guitar, Ric Holt lead guitar. Chuck Goulding played the sax, and I was not only the drummer but the lead vocalist. The other guys sang harmony or backup.

I could sing all right. We weren't the Rolling Stones, but we were a good college band.

We played frat parties on the weekends and Wednesday nights at the Clover Club in Ithaca. Sometimes we played at Syracuse. We hired a booking agent who was able to get us numerous gigs at frat parties, local clubs, and school dances in Elmira and Cortland. There were a lot of instrumental songs back then, like "Walk Don't Run" by The Ventures. And "Sleepwalk" by Santo and Johnny. That was one of our slow ones we did later in the evening, when everybody was getting ready to leave.

I survived all of this with a C average my freshman year, but when I returned as a sophomore, I began to let my class work slip. The band was playing more and more often. We opened for big acts that were passing through town like Bo Diddley, but Bo brought his own band to play with him. On big party weekends, artists like Freddie Cannon would swing through, stopping at several fraternity houses to perform.

At our house, we backed him up for a couple of his hits, "Tallahassee Lassie" and "Way Down Yonder in New Orleans."

I even got to play for Chubby Checker—back when all "The Twist" songs were really big—as part of a house band put together by our agent. That was another seven or eight dollars. They'd usually pay a band $50 to $100, and we'd split it up.

There were also more stringer assignments coming my way from newspapers. In a way, I'd developed a mini-cottage industry, making about $50 a week and having great fun doing so. By the spring semester of my sophomore year, I'd stopped going to class altogether. My grades for that semester were all "incompletes."

When I returned for my junior year, I intended to rectify my academic performance. I never did. In fact, I never even enrolled. I was back with The Hustlers, playing three or four nights a week and writing occasional pieces for out-of-town newspapers. Who needed school?

It all came to a crashing end when the tuition check for the fall semester was returned—uncashed—to my mother since I hadn't bothered to enroll. I was summoned home. My days at Cornell were over.

So I did what any down-and-out 19-year-old would have done at that moment: I got married!

Elaine Rosinus and I had been dating for about two years, ever since she'd broken up with a friend of mine. Elaine was a junior at Potsdam State Teacher's College and had taken accelerated courses, leaving only her student teaching to get her degree.

This was not good enough for her father, Walter, a widower from Germany who was adamant that Elaine get her degree before entertaining any thoughts of marriage. Looking back, I guess I wasn't a very promising prospect for a son-in-law: a college dropout without a full-time job.

Walter not only didn't walk Elaine down the aisle, he wasn't even at the wedding. He refused to be a part of it. She was given away by her maid of honor's father. My family paid for the wedding.

By then, my mother had moved to Washington, D.C., where she was the executive secretary and office manager for Senator Kenneth Keating of New York. I went down there for a couple of months to seek employment and was able to land a job with the *Washington Post*. But it wasn't the one I was after.

There were no openings in the sports department. My job at the *Post* was in merchandising and promotion, with the potential to move to sports if an entry-level position opened up. So in June 1964, Elaine and I hitched a U-Haul trailer with all of our belongings to the back of our '61 Ford Falcon and headed down to Washington to begin our life together.

Chapter **3**

Radio Days

In Washington, I went to work for the *Post* while Elaine completed her student teaching and earned her degree. The very first thing I did was write a promotional flier, an insert in the paper for Shirley Povich, the *Post*'s great sports columnist. I've still got it.

All was going well for Elaine and me, but I couldn't shake that crazy dream I had of becoming a baseball broadcaster.

Whenever I applied for a position with a radio station, there were two things—besides experience—that I lacked. I didn't have an FCC Third-Class license, which was required by most of the smaller stations. And I didn't have a professional-sounding audition tape.

In January 1965, I spotted an ad in the *Post* for the National Academy of Broadcasting. The Academy wasn't far from the paper, and during my lunch hour I walked over to find out more about it. They offered a six-month program, with classes in all phases of broadcasting. I enrolled in the evening program, and beginning in February, I went to class three nights a week after work to learn more about the profession. They taught us how to operate the equipment and the board.

When I completed the course in August, I knew I had found a career I wanted to pursue. The Academy had a job placement program and told me about an opening at a small station in Warrenton, Virginia, about 40 miles west of D.C. I scheduled an appointment and drove over one Saturday for an interview. They offered me the position that same day.

The following Monday, I gave my two-week notice to the *Washington Post*. And on Labor Day 1965, I began my broadcast career at WEER, a little 500-watt daytime station. When they said they wanted you to do everything, they weren't kidding.

I was the news director, but you did a little bit of everything. I did the morning news and sports from 6:00 AM until 10:00. From 10:00 until noon, I worked a disc jockey show. I did sales, wrote and recorded commercials, did everything from sunrise to sunset—even some play-by-play.

I was the new play-by-play man for the local high school football team, Fauquier High. Their nickname was the Fauquier ("Faw-keer") Falcons. You really had to enunciate carefully when doing those games.

A station manager from nearby Manassas, Virginia, heard my work and offered me a similar position for a little more money. So in January 1966, I moved to WPRW in Manassas. There I got a little more play-by-play experience, calling high school basketball, Little League, and American Legion baseball.

But I knew that if I wanted to do professional baseball, I first had to find work in a city that had a pro club. So I began what became a daily ritual: typing one letter and one resume, and mailing it to a station in a city that had a minor league baseball team.

Most of these letters went unanswered. But by August of that year, I had lined up about a half-dozen interviews for the week of my scheduled summer vacation. Elaine and I spent that whole week driving around upstate New York for these appointments: Rochester, Syracuse, Auburn, Binghamton, Buffalo, Elmira. From all this came one offer. In September 1966, we moved to Binghamton, New York, where I joined WNBF as a staff announcer.

Upon arriving in town, one of the first things I did was to drive out to Johnson Field, home of the Binghamton Triplets, to introduce myself to Jerry Toman, the general manager. The Triplets were a Double A affiliate of the Yankees but were not on the air and hadn't been for several years. No local station had shown any interest.

When I tried to convince my employer to carry the team's games, I was pretty much told, "If you can sell it, we can do it." But the station's sales force wouldn't be available; there weren't that many of them, and they had a full day's programming to sell.

Toman and I were convinced we could do it, but by opening day in 1967, we weren't quite there. But the WNBF management was impressed at how far we had gotten and agreed to try to sell the rest of the airtime.

About a month into the season, we were on the air—home games only.

But it was a start, and I was now a professional baseball broadcaster.

The 1968 broadcasting rights, however, went to a different station, WINR. So I followed them there. This time, it was all home games and 14 of the 70 road games. Midway through the '68 season, I was asked to pick up a newly drafted player at the airport. He turned out to be Thurman Munson.

Munson had spent part of his signing bonus on a new Corvette, which his father was driving over from Ohio. Thurman never mentioned the prickly relationship he had with his dad, but perhaps that contributed to his feisty personality.

It was evident from the start that Munson was destined for stardom. In '68, the Eastern League was the epitome of a pitcher's league. The league batting champion was Tony Torchia of Pittsfield, who hit just .294. The runner-up, his teammate Carmen Fanzone, batted .270. The highest team batting average was just .233, by Pittsfield.

But in his half-season at Binghamton, Munson hit .302 and displayed the defensive skills that made him a major league All-Star.

While I was working the Triplet games, I began to develop a reputation as someone to go to for information. I followed the game closely—reference material was always handy—and I was about the only person around who had up-to-date averages.

During those years, minor league teams didn't put out a daily stat sheet. The only stats you could get came from the league. It arrived by mail, usually on Tuesdays, and contained all of the stats for the entire league through the previous Sunday's games.

But I didn't want my listeners to be hearing stats that could be as much as a week old on the broadcasts. The local newspapers printed the Triplets box score every day, but only line scores for the rest of the league.

I was discussing this problem with John Fox, sports editor of the *Binghamton Evening Press*, when he said, "We have all the box scores. We just don't have the room to print them." From that day on, they would save these wire-service box scores and hang them in the sports department on what was labeled "Pete's Peg." Every day, I'd stop by and pick them up.

I kept a separate notebook on each team, and each day I would update the Triplets and the two or three teams they might be playing in the next week. It took time, but it was worth it. My numbers were always up-to-date.

Once players and managers for all the teams knew what I had, I became the human stat sheet.

"What's he hitting?" they'd ask. "How many strikeouts does he have? How many innings pitched? How many homers? How many steals?" I was answering dozens of questions like this every day. At the end of the season, several players came to see me and asked if they could have the game-by-game log that I'd kept of their season. I was more than happy to comply.

I remember being at the station and somebody would say, "So-and-so is here to see you." I remember one pitcher, Art Dawson, a little left-hander who wore glasses, asked me if he could see his stats.

That's the first time I heard someone say, "Ask Pete, he'll know."

We all knew that Johnson Field, built in 1913, was going to be torn down after the '68 season to make way for highway I-81. The year before, Robin Roberts, the great Phillies right-hander who won 286 games and was later inducted into the Baseball Hall of Fame, was making a comeback. He was pitching for Reading, the Phillies affiliate in the Eastern League, and trying to get back to the major leagues to win 14 more games and reach 300.

Robin was making a start at Johnson Field, and on the night before his start I had him on the pregame show. Frank Lucchesi was the Reading manager. I asked Frank if Robin was here and he said, "Yes, he'll be right out."

From the clubhouse to the dugout, you had to walk on planks of wood underneath the grandstand. It was muddy, and it was awful. It wasn't very far to go, but it was a very ugly walk. When Robin got to the dugout, he looked out over the field.

Johnson Field was a typical old minor league ballpark with bad lights and few seats. He looked out and said, "Maybe this is not such a good idea after all." And then he chuckled.

Robin pitched all right that season. In 11 starts, he pitched seven complete games and was 5–3 with a 2.48 earned-run average. He threw two shutouts, allowed just one home run, only seven walks, and had 65 strikeouts. But the Phillies didn't call him up and he decided to hang it up.

In '68, the Triplets' owners were confident that a new ballpark would be built and running by 1969. That wasn't the case, however, and after several stadium proposals fell through, the Yankees announced that they were moving the team to West Haven, Connecticut, for the '69 season.

Everyone expected it would only be a one-year hiatus. But gradually, all talk of a new stadium ceased. There were problems with location and funding, and it became a political football that no one wanted to touch, much less fumble.

I kept busy doing high school football, Broome Tech basketball games (a junior college coached by Dick Baldwin, the winningest junior-college coach of all time), and anchoring the 6:00 and 11:00 PM sports on WINR-TV.

I also hosted *Challenge Bowling*, a popular king-of-the-hill bowling show each Sunday at noon on Channel 40. The extra $30 a week was well worth it, even if it meant interviewing one champion who had no teeth. I'd ask him a question, and he'd give me an answer. To this day, I have absolutely no idea what he said.

And I still missed doing baseball.

The Yankees allowed me to come down to Yankee Stadium and tape a game that I could use as a more recent example of my work. I sent them a copy of it, asking for a critique. To my surprise, in November 1970, I got a call from Howard Berk, a Yankees vice president.

The Yankees liked my tape. They were making a change in the radio booth, and could I come to New York for an interview?

I was there the next week to meet with Michael Burke about the position. A former vice-president of CBS who, at one time, also headed the Ringling

Brothers & Barnum and Bailey Circus, Burke became the Yankees' president when CBS acquired the team.

He seemed to like my work, and the interview was going well when Burke leaned back and said, "I have only one problem—your name. I think it's a little hard to remember. Have you ever used a radio name?"

I knew what he meant. It was not that uncommon back in that era. Mel Allen was really Melvin Allen Israel. Harry Caray was born Harry Carabina. When I was growing up in Rochester, the afternoon deejay on WSAY was always called Mike Melody, even though the voice changed periodically.

But when Burke asked if I'd ever used a radio name, I replied, "No, I never have."

"What's your middle name?" he asked.

"Dirk."

Burke thought for a moment, fingers poised at his mouth, like William Buckley. Then, sounding a lot like Buckley, he said, "What about this? Peter. Peter means…the rock. Dirk? A dirk is…a dagger. What if we call you…Rock Dagger?"

I could feel myself turning beet red. Flushed with embarrassment, I began to laugh.

"I'm sorry," I said. "I can't call myself that. It just wouldn't feel right."

"Well," Burke said, "we can deal with that later. It's been very nice having you here. We'll be seeing you again soon."

All the way back to Binghamton, I kept thinking, "I'm going to be a broadcaster for the New York Yankees!"

My optimism was reinforced the next day. Jerry Toman, the Triplets former GM, called and said he'd heard from the Yankees that they were very impressed with my interview.

Within a few days, the media got wind of what was going on. I started getting calls from newspapers in Binghamton and New York City. All I could tell them was that I had been interviewed by the Yankees. What happened next I learned mostly from reading their stories.

First, I learned that the other leading candidate for the job was Don Criqui, then a CBS sportscaster. Once Criqui pulled out because the Yankees wouldn't give him September weekends off to do network football, I really thought I had the job. But I'd heard nothing from the Yankees.

At some point, Howard Cosell became involved. He'd heard former major league first baseman Bill White doing a basketball broadcast in St. Louis and recommended him to the Yankees. This also provided an opportunity for New York to hire the first black play-by-play announcer in major league history.

Just a couple of weeks before the start of spring training, White joined the Yankees broadcast team. I was told that if White had turned down the position, I would have been offered the job.

I'm so glad now that they didn't offer it to me. I was too young. I didn't have enough experience to do that job in the Yankees market.

And if it hadn't worked out, I would have been devastated.

At the time, however, I was very disappointed yet proud that I had come that close. Unfortunately, back in Binghamton, the baseball situation had not improved. A new stadium was a dead issue.

Eventually, Binghamton got its new ballpark and baseball returned, but not until 1992.

Also, we had a growing family—our son Jon was born in 1967, and Steven came in 1970—and I had pretty well maxed out my income for that market. Minor league baseball opportunities were almost non-existent then. Most Triple A clubs were broadcasting their games, but hardly any teams below that level did.

I started thinking more about simply moving to a larger market where at least the pay would be better. That opportunity came in 1972. A former colleague, Brian Kahle, had been hired by a start-up ABC-TV outlet in Toledo, Ohio. They were getting ready to launch their news operation, and they needed a sports anchor. They offered me the position with one caveat: They had a very limited budget, and the sports anchor would have to double initially as the weatherman. That September, we moved to Toledo, where I began doing double duty.

Within months, I realized I had made a mistake. The station had no budget for sports, and I really missed my first love, doing play-by-play. The Triple A Toledo Mud Hens were not even on the radio, but I was unable to get any local station to show any interest.

In February 1974, a routine trip to the Associated Press wire machine changed my life forever. A story was coming over the wire.

Marty Brennaman had been named the new radio voice for the Cincinnati Reds. Marty was the broadcaster for Triple A Tidewater, and I had met him and the team's general manager when the Tides were in Toledo.

As soon as I saw that AP story, I tore it off the wire. On the pretense of having an errand to run, I hopped in my car, drove to a nearby pay phone, and called Dave Rosenfield, the Tidewater Tides general manager. He remembered me and asked, "Do you have a tape?" I said yes, and Dave asked me to send it. I went home that night and found the one tape I had. The next day, I made a copy and mailed it to Rosey.

A few days later he called and said, "You've got the job if you want it." Boy, did I want it. "But I can't pay you what you're making now."

Boy, was he right.

I was making $18,000 a year. He was offering $10,000. Although Dave couldn't pay me what I was earning in Toledo—this was only an April-to-September position—he'd do what he could to help me find something in the off-season to supplement my income.

Without hesitating, without consulting with anybody, I said, "Yes. Yes, I'll do it." When I got home and told Elaine, she almost shot me.

She said, "You did what?! You took another job? For a pay cut of almost half? And we've got to move again?!"

"Yup, yup, yup, yes to all three," I replied. "But I promise you it will work out."

And so we were on the move once again, this time to Virginia Beach. As soon as I went to Tidewater, I had to go to spring training for my first assignment. You're from Toledo, and you had to go to spring training? Yes, that was really tough to do.

I was now doing baseball full time—every game, home and away—and I loved it. I also became close to two men who became my mentors, Dave Rosenfield and George McClelland, the sports editor of the *Virginian-Pilot*.

Rosey and I used to sit in his office for about an hour each day and just talk about baseball, broadcasting, and life. Through those conversations, I learned a lot about all three.

George and I became inseparable friends as we covered the Tides. He was a brilliant man who had incredible knowledge on a seemingly endless variety of subjects. He was also the person who pushed me the hardest to pursue my major league dreams.

As for supplementing my income, Rosenfield delivered. Of the two newspapers in the area, only one had a writer—George—that traveled with the team. The other, the *Ledger-Star*, staffed the home games (usually with Dave Lewis) but relied on wire-service accounts for road games. I became their road "beat writer." After each broadcast, I would head back to the hotel, write a story, then call the *Star* and dictate the story to a recording machine.

Rosey also helped me land a radio job broadcasting the Virginia Red Wings hockey team during the off-season. They were an affiliate of the Detroit Red Wings. I'd seen a lot of hockey growing up; I went to Rochester Americans games, and the hockey team at Cornell was great.

Since I had no hockey tape to give them, the Red Wings put me in a room with a Stanley Cup highlights film from the previous year. My audition consisted of calling play-by-play of those highlights. And I got the job. Now the one thing about it was there weren't a whole lot of hockey announcers in southern Virginia.

The 1974 Tides were not a very good team and finished last. But in '75, the Tides won the pennant and the playoffs, and they played in the Little World Series against Evansville. That Tides team featured many future major leaguers: Craig Swan, Hank Webb, Benny Ayala, Mike Vail, Roy Staiger, Bruce Boisclair, and Nino Espinosa. The manager was Joe Frazier, who later managed the Mets for a couple of seasons.

After the '75 season, it was George McClelland who called me with news that the Atlanta Braves had fired Milo Hamilton.

"Call them," George said, firmly. "Call them now!"

"But George," I said, "you know how these things are. They usually already have somebody lined up for the job when they announce something like this."

"You don't know that," he pleaded. "Call them!"

So I did. Wayne Long, the director of Braves broadcast sales, was the person who took my call.

"No, we have no replacement yet," Wayne said. "Yes, the job is wide open. By all means, send us a tape." I did.

A few days later, Wayne called back. He and Ernie Johnson, the director of broadcasting, were going to Richmond—the home of the Braves' Triple A affiliate—to call on an account, Apple Jack Chewing Tobacco. Since that was only about 90 miles from where I lived, could I drive up and meet them for an interview?

The interview went well. A few days later, they called back. The next step was to fly to Chicago (the team was still owned by Atlanta-LaSalle, a Chicago-based company) to meet with team president Dan Donohue. That day went well, too.

In early December, the telephone rang at my house. It was Ernie Johnson, and I'll never forget his words:

"How would you like to become a part of the Braves' broadcast team? You've got the job. Welcome to the Braves family."

In my professional life, I've never been any happier.

I'd only ever changed planes in Atlanta. And now I was part of the team.

Chapter **4**

A Brave New World

In December 1975, the Braves held a press conference to introduce their new broadcast team. Milo Hamilton had been fired. Ernie Johnson was the lone holdover, and the two newcomers were Skip Caray—who'd been broadcasting Atlanta Hawks basketball since 1968—and me. It was the first time I'd ever met Skip.

They had the press conference in the clubhouse in Atlanta-Fulton County Stadium. Everyone was given a card to fill out for a door prize—a Braves equipment bag. Everybody dropped their cards into the equipment bag. At some point during the press conference, someone said, "Why don't we ask the new guy to pull out the name?"

So I pulled out a card and looked at it. And I looked at it…and I looked at it. And I couldn't read the name. I couldn't read hieroglyphics. Finally, I had to ask Ernie to read it.

He was able to, but as I turned around, Skip sidled up to me, smiled, and whispered, "You're off to a helluva start, partner." And that was my introduction to Skip.

It was a year-round position with the Braves. My off-season duties included helping to sell advertising for the game program, the yearbook, and the radio network. I couldn't wait for the broadcast schedule to begin, but I had to be patient.

Our first broadcast that year was supposed to be a spring training game on March 13 between the Braves and the Los Angeles Dodgers. But a labor dispute caused a lockout, and spring training was delayed nearly three weeks.

Ted Turner, who bought the team in January 1976, couldn't wait, either. With non-roster players and minor leaguers in camp, he arranged a game with Bill Veeck, the owner of the Chicago White Sox, between the two teams featuring all non-roster players. Ted also decided to televise it.

Thus, my first broadcast with the Braves was that game on March 14 in Sarasota. You've worked in the minors for years, and you finally get a job in the major leagues. But instead of Steve Garvey, Davey Lopes, and Ron Cey of the Dodgers, or instead of the Braves' Darrell Evans, my first hitter was Jorge Aranzamendi, an infielder on the Braves' Southern League team in Savannah.

I knew these minor league guys better than Ernie did! You dream and dream about your first major league game, and that's what it turns out to be. Jorge Aranzamendi!

Eventually, spring camps opened and the season began on time. The Braves opened in San Diego. My first regular-season game took place on April 9. My first batter, Rowland Office, walked while facing Randy Jones—one of the greatest control pitchers ever. The Braves made four errors and the Padres won, 8–2, as Jones beat Carl Morton.

The next day, the Braves made big news. They announced the signing of pitcher Andy Messersmith, who'd become one of the game's first free agents and whose services were the center of a bidding war. The Braves beat out several teams by signing Messersmith to a three-year, $1 million contract.

That same day, April 10, was also when I called two other personal milestones: my first Braves' victory, a 3–0 shutout of the Padres by Phil Niekro and Pablo Torrealba, and my first major league home run call, a three-run shot by Rowland Office that decided the game.

It was a good beginning all around. The Braves won two out of three from San Diego that weekend, then went 4–3 on their first homestand of the season. The second road trip began April 23 with a win in Philadelphia.

The next morning, Ted Turner called and asked me to come to his hotel room. I couldn't imagine why he wanted to see me. I hoped it wasn't because he was unhappy with the broadcasts. When I arrived, Ted introduced me to a man named Marty who was part of the syndicate that sponsored Ted's America's Cup yacht.

"Sit down," Ted said. "Pete, when you were at Tidewater, did you travel with the team?"

"Yes," I answered.

"Did you fly or take buses?"

"Some of each, depending on how far we had to travel."

"You stayed at hotels?"

"Yes, I was with the team at all times."

"And you had buses to the ballpark?"

"Again, yes."

Ted then turned to his friend.

"What do you think, Marty? Am I doing the right thing?"

"Ted, it's your team," Marty replied. "You can do whatever you want."

Ted then picked up the phone and asked for Donald Davidson's room.

Donald was a lifelong employee of the Braves, who began as a batboy in Boston. He became traveling secretary when the Braves were in Milwaukee and despite his diminutive size—Donald was a midget—he had become an institution with the Braves.

When Donald answered the phone, Turner told him he was fired. The two were never comfortable with each other, and Ted didn't approve of Donald staying in a suite when on the road. The traveling secretary's suite was always complimentary, but Ted didn't know that.

When he hung up, Ted turned to me and said, "Van Wieren, as of now you are also the traveling secretary, in addition to your broadcast duties. We'll get you some more money when we get back to Atlanta."

"Whoa, whoa, whoa!" I responded. "I don't know anything about that job, Ted."

"Well, you'll learn," he said. "Go to Donald's room and get what you need to get us through the rest of the trip."

I felt very bad for Donald, who had treated me so well during my first months with the team—and I felt even worse when I got to his room.

Donald had obviously been crying. I told him why I was there, but he was too upset to cooperate.

"I'm not giving you anything!" he yelled, and slammed the door shut.

We had two more days in Philadelphia, then a bus trip to New York after the Sunday game. Thankfully, the buses showed up and the room keys in Manhattan were ready and waiting for us.

On Monday, I called the Braves office and spoke with Donald's secretary, Judy Maxwell. She gave me the contacts to get us home from New York.

As Ted predicted, I learned. And the position was quite complex.

The traveling secretary handles all of the elements of team travel, the hotels, the airplanes, the buses, the equipment trucks. He is responsible for the per diem payments to players on each road trip. He also handles all ticket and team official credentials for the All-Star Game, the playoffs, the World Series, and the winter meetings.

In addition, spring training is a major responsibility, getting the players there, housing them, paying their expenses. Even the spring training schedule is put together by the traveling secretary of every major league team.

This was quite a responsibility, and it made for some long days. When the Braves were playing at home, I would get to the ballpark by 10:00 AM, work on the traveling secretary business until about 4:00, then put on my broadcaster's hat and head over to the press box to prepare for that night's game.

When the season ended, it was off to the playoffs and World Series to distribute tickets and credentials—likewise for the winter meetings in December. The off-season was filled with setting up travel plans for the following year.

While rushing around and doing all of these things, a news conference called on December 17 at the stadium seemed minor: Ted was putting the WTCG signal up for satellite distribution, and the first four cities on board were Grand Island, Nebraska; Newport News, Virginia; Troy, Alabama; and Newton, Kansas.

Little did I realize what this was to become.

* * *

In 1976, the Braves began the season 8–5, then had a 13-game losing streak from which they never recovered. They finished dead last in the National

League West Division. In '77, Atlanta got off to another 8–5 start and promptly hit the skids again. After dropping both ends of a twi-night doubleheader in Pittsburgh on May 10, the losing streak had grown to 16 games, a club record.

The next morning, I got a phone call in my hotel room from Braves manager Dave Bristol. He wasn't being fired, but he was very upset. He was being given a "leave of absence" for a few days. The interim manager would be…Ted Turner! Yes. This astonishing news left me speechless. But now my role as traveling secretary kicked in.

Dave needed a flight back to Atlanta. I always carried a book of plane tickets that I could write, and I had the hotline numbers for all of the airlines. So I was able to get this done quickly.

Next problem? Dave wanted to leave the hotel without being seen. He was extremely embarrassed by this development, but he had a plan. One level below the lobby of the William Penn Hotel is a loading dock with a ramp leading up to the street level. When I delivered the plane ticket to Dave's room, he gave me his key and asked me to check him out of the hotel and take his luggage down to the loading dock where he'd meet me.

When I arrived, Dave asked me to go up to the street, hail a cab, and have it come down the ramp to pick him up. This was all to be done without anyone from the Braves traveling party seeing us. I went up the ramp but immediately spotted two familiar faces walking down the street in my direction—second baseman Rod Gilbreath and about 10 yards behind him, *Atlanta Journal* beat writer Frank Hyland.

I ran back down the ramp and told Dave what was happening. We waited while Rod and Frank passed by. Fortunately, neither one of them noticed us down at the bottom of the ramp.

Once they passed by, I walked back up the ramp, made sure no one from the team was coming, and flagged down a cab. When I told the driver about his passenger, he replied that he couldn't drive down the ramp.

His fare would have to come up to the street.

I went back down the ramp to tell Dave, but he was very wary of being seen if he walked up to the street. It was decided that I would carry Dave's luggage up the ramp, make sure the coast was clear, load the luggage into the cab, then signal him to come to the cab if no one was around.

While the puzzled cabbie looked on, I did just that—put Dave's luggage into the trunk, waved him up the ramp, got him into the cab, and sent him on his way to the airport. I felt terrible for Dave.

Then it was back into the William Penn, where the buzz was already beginning to build through the hotel about Ted managing the team. When we arrived at Three Rivers Stadium later that afternoon, it was a curious sight to see our owner in full road uniform, sitting at the desk in the visiting manager's office.

Ted had held a meeting with the coaches, delegating their responsibilities. Third-base coach Vern Benson would make all the baseball decisions offensively. Pitching coach Johnny Sain would make all of the pitching moves. Bullpen coach Chris Cannizzaro would move to the dugout, sit alongside Ted, and keep him posted on every move being made.

"Any questions?" Ted asked.

Johnny Sain raised his hand.

"Where's Dave?" he asked.

Johnny may have been the only person in Pittsburgh who'd been unaware of the day's developments.

Ted's presence didn't help that night. The Braves suffered their 17th straight loss. John Candelaria out-dueled Phil Niekro, 2–1. The Braves would have tied the game in the ninth inning on Darrell Chaney's pinch-hit double, but the ball bounced over the fence for a ground-rule double. The runner from first, Pat Rockett, who'd scored on the hit, was sent back to third.

After the game, Ted wanted something to eat. Downtown Pittsburgh had not yet undergone its revitalization, and finding a restaurant open at that late hour was not going to be easy. A group of us set out with Ted in search of a spot.

We finally found a hole-in-the-wall pizza parlor that was still open, walked in, and gave them our choices. Ted wanted a slice of cheese pizza and a glass of red wine. When the order arrived, Ted looked at it in disbelief. Instead of a triangular slice, the pizza was served as a small rectangular square. The wine came in a small juice glass.

"What is this?" Ted asked our waitress. "We didn't come here for communion!"

At least we could still laugh at the end of a long, difficult day.

Ted's managerial career lasted for one game. The next day, baseball commissioner Bowie Kuhn invoked his "in the best interests of the game" authority to remove Ted from the dugout. Vern Benson managed the team that game, and the Braves finally ended their losing streak.

Bristol rejoined the team back home in Atlanta. But once again, the Braves had dug themselves too deep a hole. The result: another last-place finish. And at the end of the year, Dave Bristol was fired.

The new manager for the 1978 season was Bobby Cox, who had been serving as a coach for the New York Yankees. I knew Bobby from the International League—he was managing Syracuse while I was at Tidewater—so it was an easy transition for me.

The Braves still weren't very good, but there were encouraging signs of improvement for the future. Dale Murphy had arrived and, after encountering some throwing problems as a catcher, had been moved to first base. On June 15 that season, the Braves acquired Gene Garber from the Phillies for Dick Ruthven, giving Atlanta a bullpen ace.

The next day, Bob Horner, the Braves' first-round draft pick out of Arizona State, made his major league debut straight out of college. In his third at-bat, Horner homered off Pirates pitcher Bert Blyleven and went on to become the National League Rookie of the Year. It wasn't enough to lift the Braves out of the cellar, but it did provide Atlanta with a rare moment in the national spotlight.

A month and a half later, there would be another, far brighter one.

On July 31, the Cincinnati Reds came to Atlanta. So did dozens of members of the media, who were all following the Pete Rose hitting streak. When Rose went 1-for-4 in the series opener, he tied the National League record of 44 consecutive games set by Wee Willie Keeler in 1897.

All eyes were on Atlanta the following night as the Braves trounced the Reds 16–4 and ended Rose's streak—12 games shy of Joe DiMaggio's major league record of 56 consecutive games. Twice Rose came close to getting a base hit—in the second inning, his line drive up the middle was speared by Braves' rookie starting pitcher Larry McWilliams. In the seventh, another Rose liner was caught by Horner and turned into a third-to-first double play.

Rose's final at-bat came in the ninth inning with two out and the bases empty. Gene Garber, bearing down, struck out Rose swinging, and I had the privilege of calling that history-making moment on TBS.

I then received instructions to stay on the air. We were going to televise—live—the postgame news conference with Rose. The TV crew scrambled to set up the live feed from a conference room in the bowels of the stadium. After a few minutes on-air, I tossed it down to the press conference.

Pete Rose didn't know that his remarks were being carried on live television. That quickly became apparent when he answered the first question.

"How do you feel now that it's over?" he was asked.

"Well, one good thing," Rose said, smirking, "I won't have to talk to you assholes every day."

While the room erupted in laughter, the telephone switchboards at TBS and the ballpark lit up. This was an era when you couldn't even say "damn" on television, and there were some very upset viewers.

Rose slipped a couple of more times during the 15-minute Q&A session, and the national media jumped all over the story. It could have been worse—it would have received an "R" rating, not an "X," had it been a movie. But if you weren't offended by the language, you got to witness—live—a truly emotional moment from one of the game's greatest players. It was honest, raw television, and because TBS was now on so many cable systems, it received national coverage.

As the '78 season ended, I was beginning to tire of my dual role with the Braves when an opportunity arose to move back into broadcasting full-time. I got a call from WITS in Boston. They had just completed their first season as the flagship station on the Red Sox radio network, but they were losing their play-by-play man, Ned Martin, who was moving to the TV side.

They flew me up to Boston for an interview. We had lunch with Rico Petrocelli, the former Red Sox star who was already on board as the radio analyst, and we talked over terms of a potential four-year deal.

I wanted to discuss the possible move with my family, and we left the offer on the table.

First, I had to travel to Toronto for the winter meetings, and I flew directly there from Boston. While at the meetings, I ran into Haywood Sullivan, the

Red Sox president. We talked about the position, and he divulged something that had not been disclosed by the station.

Unless WITS increased its nighttime signal, they would lose the broadcast after the 1979 season. I called WITS the next day and told them of my concern over this issue. They were confident their applications to the FCC for an increase in power would be approved, but it was a risk I was not willing to take. I withdrew my name from consideration.

So it was back to my dual role with the Braves, and it wasn't long into the '79 season when the gamut of emotion quickly turned—twice. On May 1, Phil Niekro recorded his 200th career victory with a win over the Pirates. After the game, Braves general manager Bill Lucas called Bobby Cox.

"Tell Phil congratulations," Bill said, "and tell him to go out and celebrate and send the bill to me."

When we returned to the hotel, the entire team was invited to a party honoring Phil in one of our suites. It was a wonderful evening. Phil's mom, Ivey, and some of his friends from nearby Ohio were there. Most of the team showed up, and we all had a terrific time. The party broke up about 1:00 AM.

At about 3:00 AM, my phone rang. It was the Greentree, Pennsylvania, police department. They had one of our players, pitcher Eddie Solomon, in custody. After leaving the party, Eddie had gone to the bar at the hotel (we had moved by then from the William Penn to the Greentree Marriott). At closing time, Eddie wouldn't leave the bar.

Hotel security was called, but when he gave them some trouble, the local police were called in. They were holding Eddie on disorderly conduct charges. They would release him to someone from the team once $50 bail was posted.

They sent a police car to the hotel to pick me up. Bail was posted, and Eddie and I were taken back to the Marriott. He begged me not to tell Bobby, but I told him I had no choice in the matter. These kinds of things had to be reported. It was around 4:30 AM by then.

At 6:30 AM, I got another call. It was horrible news—shortly after Bill Lucas had called Bobby following Phil's 200th win, Bill had suffered a massive cerebral hemorrhage and was now on life support in an Atlanta hospital.

By 8:00 AM, many of us had gathered in Bobby's suite at the Marriott. There were very few dry eyes in the room.

At the end of the 1976 season, Lucas had been named the first black general manager in major league history. After several seasons as the Braves' farm director, Lucas had put in place a plan to rebuild the Braves from within. That plan was taking shape—although the team wasn't winning yet, pieces were gradually falling into place.

But beyond his baseball abilities, Bill was one of the most likeable people in the game. His warm, friendly personality, his low-key sense of humor, and his determination to turn the Braves into a winning organization had impressed us all.

Now this. This couldn't be happening.

But it was. And a few days later, on May 5, 1979, Bill died. He was just 43.

The team never really recovered from this shocking loss. John Mullen came back to Atlanta from the Houston Astros to be the general manager, but the Braves were unable to improve their standing. They finished last in the National League West for a fourth straight year.

* * *

In 1980, the Braves finally had a winning season, their first since 1974. They went 81–80. Dale Murphy moved to the outfield and had a break-out season, batting .281 with 33 home runs and 89 RBIs. Bob Horner hit 35 homers. First baseman Chris Chambliss proved to be a valuable addition, and young players like second baseman Glenn Hubbard, shortstop Rafael Ramirez, and catcher Bruce Benedict began to establish themselves as solid major leaguers.

But for me, 1980 will always be remembered as the year I was finally able to drop traveling secretary from my job description.

One problem I frequently encountered was separating what I knew as traveling secretary from what I could say on the broadcasts. A prime example occurred in spring training of 1980. On March 22, when I arrived at my office at Municipal Stadium that morning, I was met by a plainclothes policeman from West Palm Beach, Florida.

There had been an incident outside the team hotel at about 2:00 AM the night before. Someone had fired a shot, shattering a lamppost in the hotel parking lot, and then drove off. There were witnesses, and they had given police a description of the car. The detective wanted to know where the Braves' players parked their cars.

I walked him over to the player's lot on the other side of the stadium and stayed with him as he checked out the vehicles. One car caught his attention. He peered inside the vehicle, pulled out a notebook, and checked the license plate number. Then he asked me, "Do you know whose car this is?"

I did not. So we went back to the Braves clubhouse to ask. Very quickly, we learned that the car belonged to...Eddie Solomon.

Not again, I thought.

"Could I speak to Mr. Solomon?" the officer asked.

As it turned out, he couldn't. Not at that moment. The team bus had just left for Fort Lauderdale, where the Braves were to play the Yankees, and Solomon was aboard. He was pitching that day. The officer said he'd be back later in the afternoon when the team returned.

A few minutes later, Ernie Johnson and I were in my car on our way to the game. We were broadcasting on radio that day. All the way to Fort Lauderdale, I had to keep quiet about what had just happened. I wasn't able to say anything about it during the broadcast either, or on the ride back to West Palm Beach.

When we returned, Solomon was already in our general manager's office, along with the detective, assistant GM Pat Nugent, and team president Al Thornwell. Solomon denied any involvement in the incident but admitted that he did own a gun—which he turned over to the police.

He was allowed to go; no charges were filed.

Over the next couple of days, we were informed that the investigation was expanding. There had been a similar gunshot incident earlier that same night at the Braves' minor league hotel, where Solomon had been visiting a friend. And there had been a disturbance at the airport involving someone whose description seemed to match Eddie.

This was becoming a major distraction as spring training wound down.

Braves management decided to cut their losses and traded Solomon to the Pittsburgh Pirates on March 28 for a minor league pitcher named Greg Field.

We never did hear what became of that investigation. Our friend from the West Palm Beach police stopped coming around after Eddie was gone.

I do know that someone—not the hotel—paid for repairs to the damaged lamppost.

It was the involvement in these kinds of matters that I believed I shouldn't be in the middle of as a broadcaster. I knew too much about the players: Who did and didn't pay their hotel incidentals. Who left a rental car at the hotel. Who needed a loan when they ran out of money on a road trip. There were days when I had to deal with a player over one of these issues one minute then interview him on a pregame show the next. It was not a good combination.

By the end of the year, I was nearly burned out. The stress of the dual role had created a state where I was tired all the time. I was drinking too much, and I just wanted to get away for a while.

A couple of days after the season ended, I scheduled an appointment with Ted. I had no idea how he would react when I told him I wanted to give up the travel job and concentrate on broadcasting.

"Okay," Ted said. "Do we have someone in place who can take over?"

"Yes," I answered. "Bill Acree." He was the Braves equipment manager to whom I delegated many responsibilities when the games were on the air.

"Go ahead and tell Bill," Ted said. "We'll get you some work on CNN during the off-season."

I said, "That's it? It was this easy? If I had known it would be this easy, I would have done it years ago."

That would've spared me the embarrassment of forgetting the meal money on a West Coast trip in 1976. Or the occasional travel interruptions during a broadcast.

Skip Caray, in 2000, on his broadcast partner's misadventures as a traveling secretary: "The seventh or eighth inning, Pete would get paged and turn white in the press box. The bus was late, or the plane's late, and he had to get up and leave. 'Here's the windup and the pitch, and here's Skip…'"

In the off-season, I was already doing some Atlanta Hawks broadcasts. CNN had just started, and I knew they were a little short-handed. They assigned me to a few weekend and late-night sports segments—but I was free of the travel job, and that was a great relief.

If it seems that I've devoted most of the pages covering my first five years with the Braves to traveling secretary stories, well, that's because I spent most of my time during those years doing that job. It was a huge weight off my shoulders to return to full-time broadcasting in 1981.

I know I became a better broadcaster that year simply because I could devote my full attention to it. There was more time to prepare, and when the game began, I never had to worry about buses or planes or whether all of the room keys would be ready.

The broadcasts had gone well during those five years. Ernie, Skip, and I worked very well together and our audience was growing, thanks to the rapid spread of the TBS signal to cable outlets all across the country. The widespread coverage earned the Braves the nickname "America's Team." And Braves fans were starting to show up at ballparks all across the country.

The 1981 season was interrupted in June by a players' strike. When that occurred, Ted decided to keep baseball on the air by televising the Richmond Braves. There was no other baseball on national television then, and the Richmond games actually drew higher ratings than those of the Atlanta Braves.

The Richmond games were assigned on a week-to-week basis. One week, Skip and I would call the games, the next week Ernie and Darrell Chaney would handle the duties. We would share a rental car each trip.

One morning in Richmond, I needed the car, and Skip had the keys. I called his room, but there was no answer. I knew Skip liked to sit by the pool in the morning, so I headed down there. Sure enough, there he was, lying on a chaise lounge, his back turned to me.

I walked up behind him and said, "Man, you look like a beached whale sitting out here." He rolled over and…it wasn't Skip!

I can't remember what I said next. I do remember praying that I wouldn't run into that person again during the rest of our stay.

The strike finally ended on August 10. Even though the Braves didn't make the playoffs, the ratings continued to improve.

The rise in TV ratings indirectly led to a managerial change at the end of the '81 season. Ted's television executives, led by former CBS president Bob Wussler, saw the potential for big numbers from the Braves' telecasts. They convinced Ted that the team needed a big name, a high-profile manager. Bobby Cox had not yet reached that level.

So Ted reluctantly fired Bobby—who actually showed up for the press conference announcing his firing. When asked what qualities he wanted in a new manager, Ted said, "Well, we're looking for someone just like Bobby."

Instead, Joe Torre was named the new Braves' skipper. No manager in major league history ever got off to a better start.

Chapter 5

Torre! Torre! Torre!

Like his brother Frank before him, Joe Torre played for the Braves in Milwaukee. When the Braves moved to Atlanta in 1966, Frank had retired and Joe had already made his mark as a young, slugging All-Star catcher.

In 1971, following his trade to the Cardinals, Joe hit 24 home runs for St. Louis and led the National League with 230 hits, 137 RBIs, and a .363 batting average. He was named the NL's Most Valuable Player. By 1982, Torre had retired as a player and was fired as the Mets' manager, so he returned to Atlanta to manage the Braves.

No manager had ever started as spectacularly as Joe did with the Braves.

Together, they set a major league record and set the city on fire by opening the season with 13 consecutive victories. The Braves won those 13 games in almost every imaginable way.

One win that stands out in particular came on April 14 in Cincinnati. Atlanta had won seven games in a row, but it appeared the streak was over in the bottom of the ninth in a tie game at Riverfront Stadium. With a Reds runner at second base, Paul Householder hit a screaming line drive to left-center field. But Braves left fielder Rufino Linares—never known for his defense—made a spectacular diving catch, rolled over, got to his feet, and doubled up the runner at second. The Braves scored three runs in the tenth for a 5–2 win, keeping the streak alive.

The next day, Rufino was my guest on the radio pregame show, and I asked him about the catch. He spoke limited English and had a deep, gravelly voice. His answer became one of my all-time favorites:

"He hit ball…I dive…I look over here [Rufino looked left]…No ball…I look over here [he looked right]…No ball. I look in glove…I see ball…I say, 'Rufie, you one lucky guy.'"

The Braves set a National League record with their eleventh straight win to start the year, tying Oakland's major league, season-opening mark.

Nearly 5,000 people greeted the team when it returned to Hartsfield Airport. One sign said: "Torre! Torre! Torre!—162–0"

Back home in Atlanta, the Braves kept winning, and the town went wild again. The team gave out commemorative 8"x10" placards after the next win, keepsakes of the 4–2 victory over Cincinnati for the record-breaker:

I Was There…

12

Atlanta Braves vs. Cincinnati Reds

Atlanta-Fulton County Stadium

Atlanta, Georgia. April 20, 1982

The streak finally reached 13 before a 2–1 loss to the Reds. Even after it ended, the Braves continued to walk away with the division. By July 29, the team had opened up a nine-game lead over the Dodgers.

But then a complete reversal of fortune came along. The Braves lost 19 of their next 21 games and fell into second place, four games behind LA.

After the double-header loss in Montreal that dropped the Braves four games behind, infielder Jerry Royster boarded the team bus. In an effort to loosen up his teammates, Jerry said:

"Boys, we've got them [the Dodgers] right where we want them."

Entering the final week of the regular season, the Braves still trailed Los Angeles by three games. But a 5–2 West Coast road trip that concluded in San Diego and a collapse by the Dodgers gave Atlanta its first NL West division title since 1969. Joe Morgan's three-run home run for San Francisco on the final day of the season gave the Braves the division by the slimmest of margins—one game.

The team flew straight from San Diego to St. Louis to open the NLCS.

On that flight, Dale Murphy, who was about to win his first Most Valuable Player award, went up to every player and recalled a game where that player had been the key to a victory.

It was a great example of how humble, how "aw shucks" Murph was. He walked up and down the aisle and went to every single player on that team and said, "Hey Joe, you remember that game with the Phillies when you hit that home run in the seventh and we won? That's the game that won it for us."

Or he'd say, "Remember that game you pitched against the Mets? That's the game that won it for us." That's the kind of guy Murph was. He tried to make *every* player feel special. So typical. He never wanted to be the guy everyone singled out.

The series in St. Louis is best remembered for one thing: the rain.

Game 1 was halted after 4½ innings with the Braves leading 1–0 behind Phil Niekro. There were two outs in the bottom of the fifth inning when play was stopped. It rained and rained until the game was finally called. Commissioner Bowie Kuhn didn't want a playoff game decided in just five innings.

It took four days to get in the two scheduled games. The night after the Game 1 rainout, St. Louis won easily and later rallied to win Game 2, 4–3. The Cardinals completed the three-game sweep in Atlanta with a 6–2 victory to win the pennant.

Despite the disappointing ending, the season was a spectacular success. TBS ratings soared. *Sports Illustrated* did an article on Braves fans in Storm Lake, Iowa; Valdez, Alaska; and Reno, Nevada. Our fan mail was pouring in from all over the world, and Braves fans were showing up in virtually every ballpark on the road.

In succeeding years, the team's popularity continued to increase—but the performance slipped and then plummeted. After a second-place finish in 1983 (four games behind the Dodgers), and a more distant runner-up finish in '84 (12 games behind San Diego), the front office decided to make another managerial change.

This time the baseball people got their way. Longtime minor league manager Eddie Haas got the job. It not only didn't work out, Eddie didn't even finish the season. He was the manager for 121 games and went 50–71.

Eddie was a good baseball man, but he hated talking to and dealing with the media. At Shea Stadium one day, Eddie came up to me in the clubhouse and, pointing to the visiting manager's office, said, "Pete! Pete! Who are all those people in there?" I said, "It's the New York media." It was Red Foley, Jack Lang, and all of the New York writers.

Eddie said, "I don't want 'em in there. Get 'em outta there!" I said, "Eddie, I can't do that. I'm part of the media."

Bobby Wine took over as interim manager in August after Haas was fired. It didn't help. The Braves fell into last place and finished 30 games under .500 with a 66–96 record.

During the 1984 season, another team approached me about a broadcast opening. The St. Louis Cardinals were in town, and Jack Buck called me aside. They were going to make a change in 1985, Jack said, and he wanted to know if I had any interest.

We talked for a couple of days. But since the money was the same as what I was already earning, I decided against making the lateral move.

As the Braves were crashing back toward the division cellar, two of the most memorable games of my career occurred. The first was August 12, 1984, when Atlanta hosted the San Diego Padres. The game began with Pascual Perez hitting Padres leadoff batter Alan Wiggins with a pitch.

The teams then began trading retaliatory knockdown pitches. By the end of the day, we witnessed several brawls (one involved a couple of overzealous fans), resulting in the ejections of 19 players, coaches and both managers. A tape of this game is kept in the Braves clubhouse to this day, and it makes for an eye-popping show for those who have never seen it.

The game that etched itself into my memory was the July 4, 1985, night game against the New York Mets in Atlanta-Fulton County Stadium. That game, too, is often replayed on ESPN Classic and the MLB cable channel.

It went 19 innings. There were more than three hours of combined rain delays. In the eighteenth inning, after the Mets had taken an 11–10 lead, Braves pitcher Rick Camp came to bat. Never mind that he was a career .060 hitter. There were no Atlanta position players left to pinch-hit for a reliever.

Incredibly, Camp somehow homered to left field, and the game went into the nineteenth inning. And what was left of a good-sized Fireworks Night crowd went crazy. In the nineteenth, the Mets scored five runs off Camp; the Braves responded with two in the bottom half and lost 16–13. Then, at 4:00 AM on July 5, the July 4 fireworks show began—and frightened the entire neighborhood. I also recall that we had a game that afternoon at 2:30. So we had to sleep fast.

For much of the 1980s, Dale Murphy was arguably the most dominant player in the National League. He was voted the National League's Most Valuable Player in 1982 and again in '83. In 1985, Murphy led the league with 37 home runs (following three straight 36-homer seasons) and recorded his fourth straight 100 RBI season. From 1980–87, he was a seven-time NL All-Star and often the only reason to watch the Braves.

By the late '80s, though, even Murphy was in decline.

The years 1986 through 1990 seemed like one long, losing season. The Braves had reverted to their mid- to late-seventies form. They finished at or near the bottom of the division every year. In 1986, 89 losses. 92 more in 1987. 106 in '88. And 97 defeats in '89 and again in '90.

Chuck Tanner was hired as the new manager in October 1985.

After taking Toronto to the 1985 American League playoffs, Bobby Cox resigned as the Blue Jays manager and returned to Atlanta as the Braves general manager. While Bobby was unable to get the major league club turned around, he did set the foundation for the 14-year run of division titles that began in 1991.

When he was re-hired by the Braves as the GM, Bobby told everyone it would take five years to retool the organization. He was right.

Minor league affiliates were added, as were more coaches and minor league instructors. The size of the scouting staff increased, and a number of trades were made with an eye on the future.

During that five-year span, the Braves acquired a half-dozen key players in deals: Pete Smith, John Smoltz, Jeff Treadway, Francisco Cabrera, Charlie

Liebrandt, and Marvin Freeman. Each year's free-agent draft added to the talent pool; with Kent Mercker in 1986, Brian Hunter and Mike Stanton in '87, pitchers Steve Avery and Mark Wohlers in 1988, Ryan Klesko in '89, and Chipper Jones in '90.

The future was bright. There were, however, only a few highlights for the major league club during this time.

On July 6, 1986, Bob Horner became just the eleventh player in major league history to hit four home runs in a game. The first three came off Montreal starter Andy McGaffigan, the fourth came off reliever Jeff Reardon.

I had the call of the historic fourth home run—but no one saw it live. July 6 was also the opening day for the first-ever Goodwill Games in Moscow. The event was the brainchild of Ted Turner. All of the television coverage aired on TBS.

That first day, a Sunday, Goodwill Games programming was scheduled from noon to 6:00 PM (EDT) and from 8:00 PM to midnight. The Braves telecast was tape-delayed and edited down to the two-hour window from 6:00 to 8:00 PM.

The drama of Horner's accomplishment was lost by then, as was the game. Despite the historic four-homer performance, the Braves lost to Montreal 11–8.

In 1987, Dale Murphy had a career power year, hitting 44 home runs.

Yet the Braves still lost 92 games. More typical of that season was the day pitcher Randy O'Neal had to be scratched from a scheduled start in Cincinnati. He had fallen asleep poolside at the team hotel and was badly sunburned.

The 1988 record was even worse, 54–106, as the Braves finished 27 games behind fifth-place Houston in the NL West. Chuck Tanner was fired after a 12–27 start that included 10 straight losses to open the season. Russ Nixon took over, but the club didn't play any better for him.

The best story from that season came during spring training. Graig Nettles, the 43-year-old former Yankees star, had spent the 1987 season with the Braves and was trying to win a spot on the roster in '88. When he arrived at Municipal Stadium in West Palm Beach on March 24, the first thing Nettles did was leave a ticket for his wife for that afternoon's game with the Montreal Expos.

A couple of hours before game time, Nettles was sold to the Expos.

Since both teams trained at the same facility, all Nettles had to do was pack up his gear and take it to the Montreal side of the complex.

The Expos immediately penciled Nettles' name into the starting lineup. They knew he could play third base, but they wanted to take a look at him at first base, too.

When the Expos took the field, Graig heard a familiar voice from behind the Braves' dugout.

"Graig…Graig…What happened?"

He'd had no time to call his wife.

"Tell you later," he responded.

By mid-season, the Braves were looking for something, anything to give the fans a reason to come to the ballpark. They thought they'd found it when they purchased pitcher German Jimenez from the Mexican League.

We were told that Jimenez could be the next Fernando Valenzuela, but it didn't quite work out that way. Jimenez went just 1–6 with a 5.01 ERA.

One oddity about that experiment was that whenever German pitched, his wife and young son (about 3) came to the game. For some reason, they never went to the family lounge before the game began but always came to the press lounge. Even after they were shown where the family lounge was located, they still came upstairs to the press level. Maybe the food up there was better.

The 1989 season was marked by a drastic decline in Dale Murphy's performance. The two-time MVP and seven-time All-Star hit just .228, with only 20 homers, and we began to hear rumors that Murphy might be traded. It finally happened on August 3, 1990, in Houston.

Murphy's name was not in the starting lineup that evening, but we thought he was just getting a night off. Braves vice president Hank Aaron happened to be in town to do an autograph signing. He came to the Astrodome that evening. About 15 minutes before game time, he stuck his head into our radio booth and asked us, "How do you like the deal?"

"What deal?" we asked.

"Murphy," Aaron said.

The trade to the Phillies wasn't officially announced until about the fourth inning during the game. But we had been able to alert our listeners that a deal was imminent, thanks to Hank's tip.

The Braves had been seeking a power partner for Murphy since Bob Horner had left to play in Japan in 1987. They thought they had found one when they signed Nick Esasky as a free agent. In 1989, Esasky had hit 30 home runs and driven in 108 runs for the Boston Red Sox.

But shortly after the 1990 Braves season began, Esasky began suffering dizzy spells. He was diagnosed with vertigo. In nine games, he was 6-for-35 with 14 strikeouts and no extra-base hits. Esasky never played for Atlanta, or in the major leagues, again.

This just added to the list of disappointments the Braves suffered during the late 1980s. Ken Griffey Sr. didn't have much left when they got him. Jody Davis was a flop. There was German Jimenez. And now Nick Esasky.

Yet a nucleus of young, talented players was growing. In 1987, Tom Glavine, Pete Smith, Jeff Blauser, and Ron Gant arrived. In '88, it was John Smoltz and Mark Lemke. In '89, pitchers Mike Stanton and Kent Mercker joined the bullpen. And in 1990, left-handed pitcher Steve Avery and David Justice, who was named the National League Rookie of the Year, arrived. That helped diffuse some of the fans' anger after Murphy was traded.

Bobby Cox had taken on a dual role earlier that season, moving back down to the field after manager Russ Nixon was fired in June following a 25–40 start. A new general manager would be hired in the off-season, and Bobby would concentrate on managing. At the time, no one could have imagined just how great those moves and that pairing would prove.

Throughout the 1980s, we also went through a series of changes in the broadcast booth. After the 1980 season, management decided to add a fourth broadcaster to the mix, giving us a two-man team on both radio and TV.

That fourth man changed over the years, seemingly at management's whim. First, they wanted another ex-player. Darrell Chaney was brought aboard. After the 1982 season, they wanted more of a play-by-play man in that fourth spot, and John Sterling replaced Chaney. Later in the '80s, they leaned back toward the ex-player. So Billy Sample was hired for a couple of seasons before being dropped in 1989 for Don Sutton.

Sutton's arrival came the same year that Ernie Johnson surprised us by announcing his retirement. Despite the Braves' poor play, a sellout crowd filled Atlanta-Fulton County Stadium on September 2. It was Ernie Johnson Night at the ballpark, and the fans who loved Ernie really showed their appreciation that night.

Ernie had announced his retirement in mid-season. On that night in September, the game was sold out. That's what people thought of him.

We were all happy for Ernie, but we also knew how much we would miss him.

Chapter **6**

Changing Times

By the end of the 1990 season, the Braves had become a rather predictable team. In my first fifteen years as a Braves broadcaster, I had seen only three winning seasons, eight last-place finishes and, except for that unexpected spike in 1982, no postseason action at all. That changed dramatically in 1991.

There were other changes occurring at about the same time, changes that reduced the visibility of the players when they were not on the field.

When I first came to Atlanta prior to the 1976 season, one of the first events I attended was the Eddie Glennon Gameboree. It was an annual banquet hosted by the Braves 400 Club, the original fan club founded when the Braves moved to Atlanta from Milwaukee.

This was a huge event held annually a few weeks before the start of spring training. Nearly all of the players attended, in addition to stars from other teams—Jim Rice, Dave Parker, even Orioles manager Earl Weaver one year. A three-tiered head table, or dais, was not uncommon.

But by 1990, the magnitude of this event had diminished. Few if any players showed up. In fact, the focus of the event gradually changed to honoring Braves alumni and minor league stars. This was happening all over the country. Just about every major league city had an annual off-season baseball bash. Only a handful do now.

It's hard to pinpoint why these events all but disappeared, but I believe the onset of agents is partly to blame. Today's players get paid extra for almost everything they do off the field, and booster clubs don't have that kind of spending power.

Another great tradition that has all but disappeared is the promotional tour that took place in the off-season—the annual Braves Caravan. This was a week-long jaunt, usually in January, included 15 to 20 players, team executives, the broadcasters, and the manager. We would meet in Atlanta, load up two RVs and head out on a Sunday evening.

One group would drive north, perhaps to Richmond or Charlotte, and then start working its way back toward Atlanta through Tennessee, the Carolinas, and north Georgia. The other RV would drive south, usually to Jacksonville and cover northern Florida, south Georgia, and Alabama.

Eventually, both groups would converge back in Atlanta the following Saturday at a mall like Northlake Mall. They'd have a big autograph show with big posters with everybody's picture on it, which we would sign for the fans. Then that night, we'd attend the Gameboree.

The itineraries and cities we visited changed every year, and the schedule was incredibly diverse. There were visits to hospitals and schools, autograph sessions at shopping malls, luncheons for civic groups like the Rotary and Kiwanis clubs, media interview sessions, and special appearances at a wide variety of events. We even went to the space center in Huntsville, Alabama. That was cool.

One year, my Caravan group had an interesting stop in Nashville. We met with the governor of Tennessee, Lamar Alexander, and we all posed for a photo in the state capitol. We later toured the Grand Ole Opry and were guests that evening at Boots Randolph's club on Printer's Alley.

Boots was apparently not a big baseball fan. He introduced us to the audience as "Bobby *Fox* and his *Atlantic* Braves!"

One year in the early 1980s, when Joe Torre was the manager, we had an overnight stay in Anniston, Alabama, which included dinner at a local hotel. During dinner, a photographer from the local newspaper snapped some photos of our table. Then he told Torre, "I need the names of every person at the table." This included the police officer sitting with us.

Joe complied, identifying the players and me. But when he got to the policeman, whose name he didn't know, Joe said, "And one of your local gendarmes."

The next morning's paper ran the photo, and the caption identified each member of the Braves' party—except for that policeman, who was called "Officer John Darmes."

We were all laughing about that as we pulled out of Anniston. That's when the local radio station aired a portion of an interview they had done the night before with pitcher Al Hrabosky—"The Mad Hungarian," as he was called. Al was in a playful mood while giving that interview—and he was stunned to hear that his tongue-in-cheek remarks about growing up in Czechoslovakia and playing in the Prague Little League actually aired.

The weather brought our Caravan to a halt one winter when an ice-storm left us stuck in a downtown Chattanooga hotel for two days.

We whiled away the time playing cards or taking our turns at the Pac-Man game in the lounge. By the second day, though, we were getting pretty antsy.

Our PR rep on that trip heard about a senior citizens home just a couple of blocks from our hotel and asked if we wouldn't mind walking over to pay them a visit. We happily agreed, and off we went.

Rick Camp and Darrell Chaney had been having fun on that particular Caravan with a whoopee cushion and brought it along to the senior center. When we entered a large recreation room and were introduced to a dozen or so residents, Rick decided to put the cushion to good use.

He sat down next to one of the women and when she heard the noise, her face reddened and she said, "Oh, I'm so sorry." Phil Niekro started laughing so hard he had to leave the room.

We really had fun on those Caravans. Not only did we do some PR and spread some goodwill on those trips, but it was also a real good way for the manager and players to get to know each other. For them to bond in a setting that wasn't a game situation. There were B.S. sessions, or we would watch movies, have some drinks, get to know each other—the broadcasters, too.

On one trip, when Russ Nixon was the manager, Pete Smith found out he'd be the Opening Day starting pitcher during a press conference at one of the stops. A media member asked Russ, "Have you picked out your Opening Day starter yet?"

Russ looked down at Pete, who was sitting right next to him, and said, "I think you're looking at him."

The Caravan was also how Bobby met his wife, Pam, at the mall in Rome, Georgia. Bobby walked into a Belk's store where she worked. They started going out and, a year later, got married.

At the end of the Caravan week, there would be a big autograph show at one of Atlanta's malls. By this time, everyone was a little punchy from the two-cities-a-day schedule we'd been on all week. A classic example occurred one year in the early 1980s.

At that autograph session, a very attractive teenage girl, with her mother in tow, came through the autograph line. Several of us were sitting at the table and signing, including Steve "Bedrock" Bedrosian. The girl was too shy to speak for herself, so her mother spoke up.

"Oh, Mister Bedrosian! You're my daughter's favorite ballplayer!" the mother said. "It would mean so much to her to have your autograph. Would you sign my daughter's jeans?"

"Sure," Steve said.

So the girl turned around and sat on the table, and Bedrock signed one of her back pockets.

The girl was still speechless, but the mother seemed more excited than her daughter.

"Oh, Mister Bedrosian, thank you so much!" the mother squealed. "She'll never take those jeans off again!"

"She will if she goes out with me," Steve said.

This time, it was Bruce Benedict and I who had to get up and walk away from the table for awhile before we finally stopped laughing.

At a high school in Sumter, South Carolina, we did a morning assembly program. The assembly ran long and we had to be at the Chamber of Commerce at noon. Once we got down to the Chamber lunch, we realized we'd left someone back at the school—Rally, the Braves mascot.

"I'll go back and get him," a state trooper said. Rally was supposed to start the program. All of a sudden, we heard a siren. Rally was in the trooper's car and had put on his uniform. All you could see in the back seat of the car was this big baseball head.

We had so much fun on those Caravans, but by 1990 it was getting tougher and tougher to get players to participate. The per diem allowance was no longer an incentive for these high-priced athletes. Many were into their preseason workout schedule as early as January and didn't want to disrupt that. And the Braves' popularity on the TBS Superstation was drawing crowds that were, at times, unmanageable. We were on a tight schedule, and an autograph show at a mall would normally run two hours. But when 2,000 people showed up, there'd be a line as long as you could see. They'd have to tell everyone, "One item only." But even then, about 1,000 of them went away empty-handed and angry.

By 1992, the Caravans ended. Nowadays, you can't get players to go on them. They did resume, however, although on a much smaller scale. Today, it's a player or two, a broadcaster, and maybe a team executive or the manager on a one-city one-day trip.

The big off-season promotion now takes place at Turner Field, usually over a two-day weekend. The "Fanfest," as it's called, raises money for the Braves Foundation, a charitable wing of the organization. Most players are willing to show up for that.

* * *

The boom in the baseball memorabilia business has also played a role in the reluctance of players to participate in caravan-like events.

One of the last big Caravans conducted by the Braves was held in Columbia, South Carolina, in a big building at the state fairgrounds. They held a fund-raising banquet for a children's hospital, and it was very well attended. Some 300-400 people were there. We took questions from the audience. After dinner at the end of the evening, the crowd could bring up their programs to get them autographed by the players.

It wrapped up around 10:00 PM, and one of the organizers asked us if we'd mind sticking around for a few more minutes to sign items to be auctioned off for charity. We said yes. They had boxes and boxes of baseballs, a dozen balls in each box, maybe ten dozen balls total. They also had pictures and posters of the players who were there.

Guys started signing, and it was taking longer than a few minutes. We didn't get out of there until 11:00 PM. No one was really upset, but we said, "That took a long time."

When we were leaving the next morning, we drove by a strip mall. A sandwich-board sign sat outside a sports memorabilia store that said, "Just Arrived: Braves Autographed Items." I wonder where they got those? That really irritated the players, Tom Glavine and Pete Smith in particular.

There's a lot of people who get very miffed when a player won't sign autographs. Players don't mind signing autographs for kids or fans. But those memorabilia dealers…

One day in Philadelphia, there were mostly young kids waiting outside our hotel before the bus left for the ballpark. There was also a limo sitting there, waiting. Bill Acree, our traveling secretary, asked the valet parking attendant to ask the driver to move the limo. It was right where our team bus needed to pull up.

The valet guy told Bill, "I can't ask them that."

It turns out there are some memorabilia companies that are owned by, shall we say, people who are connected. They thought they were getting stiffed by some of these kids, who might have been keeping some of the autographed items for themselves. So they had guys sitting in the limo, watching the kids.

In New York, where we stayed at the Grand Hyatt, there were always lots of guys standing outside, waiting for players to come out and board the bus to the ballpark. They weren't just fans or autograph hounds but guys getting memorabilia items signed for resale. That's why some players would leave early for the ballpark and just hire a car service before the autograph guys got there.

One time outside the Grand Hyatt, there was a guy with posters of all the 300 game winners. He asked Don Sutton to sign it. Don asked him to come inside with him and have a drink. What Don was trying to figure out was if this guy was a memorabilia dealer. The guy said, "Okay, I'll pay you $200 to sign it." Don said okay.

That's the kind of thing that's killing autographs for children. But if this guy is going to sell something for $5,000, the players should get something. There are certainly correct ways to go about it, and the legitimate dealers do it right: "We'll pay you $500 to sign ten dozen baseballs."

Now there are going to be fans who'll read this and say, "The players make enough money." That's not the point. The Beatles still make a lot of money, and they haven't been together for nearly 40 years.

Chapter **7**

Worst to First

It was the best of times, the worst-to-first of times. Baseball culture in Atlanta changed forever in 1991. It was the greatest season imaginable, the greatest in franchise history and the city's history. So many things happened that year. It is still considered the greatest season and probably always will be.

It was the year of the Tomahawk Chop, the Chant, the greatest turnaround in baseball history, and the greatest World Series ever.

We knew the Braves would be much improved from 1990 after all the changes the team had made. Bobby Cox had moved down to the dugout for good to manage many of the young players the organization had signed and developed in the minor leagues while he was the general manager.

The new GM, John Schuerholz, came from a successful reign in Kansas City and made significant moves in the off-season to shore up weak areas on the team. He acquired three veterans, third baseman Terry Pendleton from St. Louis, and first baseman Sid Bream and shortstop Rafael Belliard from Pittsburgh—to improve what was the National League's worst defense (158 errors in 1990) and to provide veteran leadership.

To improve the club's speed, Schuerholz added Deion Sanders to the roster and traded a couple of minor leaguers to the Montreal Expos for outfielder Otis Nixon. To shore up the bullpen, Juan Berenguer—"Señor Smoke"—was signed.

The starting pitching was already there: Tom Glavine, John Smoltz, Charlie Leibrandt, Steve Avery and Kent Mercker. All but Leibrandt had been brought up through the Braves' system.

When spring training began, Pendleton and Bream immediately went to work on creating a more positive attitude in the clubhouse. On the field, the evolution of the worst-to-first season began with some fans having some innocent fun.

When Deion Sanders, the lightning-quick two-sport star from Florida State, came to the plate during spring training, Seminole fans in the crowd—there are always a few in Florida—began doing the FSU football chop and war chant always seen and heard in Tallahassee on fall football Saturdays. If Deion got a base hit, they would sometimes continue with the next hitter.

It wasn't a big deal, just something cute that was going on during spring training. When Deion made the ballclub, the Florida State connection brought the chop and chant to Atlanta. But it was still mostly reserved for Deion and limited to a few fans.

But as the season progressed, more and more fans were getting in on the act and were chopping and chanting whenever the Braves began to rally. John Schuerholz noticed this phenomenon and urged stadium organist Carolyn King to prompt the crowd with the chant music whenever appropriate.

But it was still an ongoing experiment.

At the All-Star break, the Braves were a little better than previous years—the team finished last four of the previous five seasons. The won-lost record was 39–40, but they were still 9½ games behind the Los Angeles Dodgers in the NL West.

At that point, Bobby Cox made a key managerial decision. John Smoltz was 2–11, and his struggles had many believing that he should be removed from the starting rotation. The Braves had even engaged a sports psychologist, Jack Llewellyn, to work with Smoltz.

When Smoltz was pitching, Llewellyn would always be sitting in the stands directly behind home plate and wearing a red shirt to give Smoltz a point of focus. This worked everywhere but St. Louis, where everybody wore red shirts. But the association had the desired effect.

Smoltz became a key element in what was about to happen.

Immediately after the break, Atlanta went 9–2 with Smoltz picking up three of those wins, while the Dodgers slumped to 2–9. Suddenly, the Braves were in a pennant race. Suddenly, chopping and chanting were becoming more and more *en vogue*.

Enter Paul Braddy, an Atlanta entrepreneur, who saw a chance to make some money from this new fad. He manufactured some foam-rubber tomahawks to be sold at Braves concession stands. Initially, sales were flat.

The chop and the chant were catching on, but most fans simply used their arms when chopping.

All that changed on Saturday, September 14. The Braves had pulled within a half-game of Los Angeles and were hosting the Dodgers in a nationally televised Game of the Week on CBS. The Braves had cut a deal with a local sponsor, UNOCAL, to give a free foam-rubber tomahawk to each fan. A sellout crowd of 44,773 took their seats, fully armed.

In the bottom of the ninth, with the score tied 2–2, Otis Nixon singled and was sacrificed to second by Lonnie Smith. Terry Pendleton was intentionally walked by Jim Gott, and that brought up David Justice.

This time, no prompting was necessary.

Suddenly and spontaneously, the entire crowd erupted in an a cappella chant. It could be heard at a Morehouse College football game more than a mile away. In the radio booth, Don Sutton and I stared at each other in amazement. You couldn't help but get chills. It sounded like the Mormon Tabernacle Choir times ten, and the sight of 40,000 orange tomahawks (the sponsor's color) chopping in unison was indescribable.

Justice was so startled he had to step out of the batter's box and survey the incredible scene. At his Braves Hall of Fame induction in 2007, when I asked him about this, David told me, "That is still one of the most memorable moments of my career."

Justice struck out, but that hardly mattered. When the Braves won the game 3–2 in the eleventh inning on a Ron Gant base hit, they moved into first place. And a new Braves tradition was born. That was really the birth of the chant being our war cry.

Over the next couple of weeks, we were inundated with hundreds of homemade tomahawks that we received in the mail. Wooden tomahawks. Knit tomahawks. Even an electric neon tomahawk. The phenomenon attracted network television news coverage across the country.

For the rest of the pennant race and at every home game in the NLCS and the World Series, I went to the ballpark early every day to see what would happen. I went up and walked the entire concourse that encircled the stadium, looking out into the parking lots to watch and listen.

There were people everywhere, tomahawks everywhere. There were Indians beating their drums. There were Native American protestors in the postseason, demonstrating against the chop and the chant and the Braves' nickname. There was music and just so much excitement going on every game. I didn't want to miss a thing because I didn't know if it would ever happen again.

Our TV ratings on TBS soared. We were getting up to a 40 share—40 percent of the audience—locally, and we were showing up in the national ratings with shares as high as 7.

On the road, fans were traveling from all over to chop and chant and cheer for the Braves. A weekend series in Houston in late September saw Braves fans far outnumbering Astros fans at the Astrodome by almost a 2-to-1 margin.

In the standings, the Braves and Dodgers kept swapping places at the top of the division. And every game seemed to have a different hero, a different story.

One of my favorites occurred on October 1 in Cincinnati. With only five games left in the season, the Braves had fallen a game behind the Dodgers. When the Reds struck for six runs in the first inning that night at Riverfront Stadium, it looked grim for Atlanta. But the Braves nibbled back against José Rijo. By the ninth inning, they'd pulled back to make it a 6–5 game.

With Rob Dibble, Cincinnati's hard-throwing relief ace on the mound, Justice—who'd grown up in the Cincinnati area as a Big Red Machine fan—hit a dramatic two-run homer to give Atlanta a 7–6 lead. The Braves held on to win and tied the Dodgers for the NL West lead.

Watching all this on television in Greenville, South Carolina, was a veterinarian named Ed Moseley. When Justice connected in the ninth, Moseley began screaming, "Get out! Get out!" That awakened his wife, Kathleen, who was asleep upstairs.

Mrs. Moseley quickly dialed 911, thinking that an intruder had broken into the house. A few minutes later, when a policeman—with blue lights flashing on his car—pulled into the Moseleys' driveway, Ed had to sheepishly explain that he'd been yelling at the television about a homer, not a home invader.

By October 5, the season had wound down to the final two games, and the Braves held a one-game lead over the Dodgers. That Saturday, before another sellout crowd in Atlanta-Fulton County Stadium and behind the pitching of John Smoltz, the Braves beat the Astros, 5–2, to clinch at least a tie for the division title. I'll never forget seeing Greg Olson pull off his catcher's mask, race toward the mound, and leap into Smoltz's arms.

My call of the final out:

"One ball, two strikes. The stretch by Smoltz, the pitch to Cedeno…high fly ball, right field. It's fairly deep. Back goes Justice…he's got it! And the magic number for Atlanta is down to one!"

I wasn't scheduled to work the ninth inning, and Skip wasn't even there. He was out of town, preparing to call a football game for TNT. Skip's son, Chip, was supposed to call the ninth. Instead, he said on the air:

"There's a couple of guys [meaning Skip and myself] who have waited nearly ten years for this opportunity. So it's only apropos as we go the top of the ninth…here's Pete."

Then Chip stood up and left the booth. That was very classy of him to let me call that ninth inning, and it's something I'll always appreciate.

As our game ended, out in San Francisco the Dodgers were in the top of the ninth with two outs and trailing the Giants 4–0. We stayed on the air to report on that game while Bobby Cox, the coaches, and players gathered on the mound to watch the Dodgers game on the big video screen in center field.

When Eddie Murray grounded out to Robby Thompson, it was over.

My call:

"The Braves are the National League West champions! The San Francisco Giants have just beaten the Los Angeles Dodgers 4–0! Let the celebration begin, Atlanta!"

The team erupted in celebration on the field. The crowd went wild. My sons, Jon and Steve, were driving back from a Georgia football game in Athens and were listening to the Braves game on the radio. They later said that after the final out, everyone driving on the highway out of Athens started honking their horns, waving little Braves flags, and doing the chop out their car windows.

That celebration permeated the entire city. Office buildings displayed good luck signs. Tomahawk flags adorned mailboxes all over Atlanta. The chant was heard on every radio station in town.

On Monday, our motorcade was heading from the ballpark to the airport for our flight to Pittsburgh. We not only had a police escort but some unexpected roadside support, too. As our three buses drove by, a road gang of jail inmates stopped doing their work and started doing the chop. On our bus, people laughed and pointed out the window and said, "Look at that!"

Once at the airport, we were given a sendoff by a crowd estimated at 5,000 fans. They chopped and chanted to the music of the Fort McPherson Army Band.

Catcher Greg Olson's "Playoff Diary" quickly became required reading. Each day, Oly would speak to a *Journal-Constitution* reporter and tell him about the previous game and that day's itinerary. Greg never failed to get in plugs for everything: Where he and his family ate, the rental car company that gave his parents a good rate, the doughnut shop that gave Oly a free dozen.

As Game 1 of the National League Championship Series began, I looked over at the Pittsburgh radio booth and nodded at Pirates broadcaster Lanny Frattare. I had known Lanny since he was about three years old.

He grew up about ten blocks from me in Rochester. His dad started the Little League where I first played. At the start of each season, we would go to the Frattare home to pick up our uniform and a bat; Lanny was in charge of the bats.

We both went to the same high school and both followed similar career paths. Lanny worked in Geneva, New York, then Rochester and Charleston, West Virginia, before landing with the Pirates in 1976—the same year I started with the Braves. Now here we were, side-by-side in Three Rivers Stadium for the NLCS. What are the odds of that?

After Game 1, a 5–1 loss in which Doug Drabek beat Tom Glavine, I remember I.J. Rosenberg's lead in the *Atlanta Journal-Constitution* the next morning:

"The Atlanta Braves came to the city of steel confident they were ready for a playoff showdown against the club with the major leagues' best record.... But when the CBS cameras clicked on Wednesday night and all of the baseball world turned their eyes on the Braves, they froze like an actor with stage fright."

It basically said, "The Braves choked." Everybody saw that. It was put up in the Braves clubhouse, and everybody read it—and everybody was angry.

In Game 2, Steve Avery out-dueled former Brave Zane Smith, winning 1–0. Avery threw 8⅓ scoreless innings and struck out nine. Afterward, Pirates centerfielder Andy Van Slyke gave Ave a new nickname: Poison Avery.

Back home in "the Chop Shop," as Atlanta-Fulton County Stadium had come to be known, the Braves pounded Pittsburgh 10–3 in Game 3. Greg Olson had a lot of baseball fodder for his daily diary. Not only did he hit a two-run home run—his first homer in two months—he even stole the third base of his career.

When Olson was holding court in the clubhouse afterwards, a local TV guy said, "Who does he think he is, Johnny Bench?"

"He was today," said Braves coach Pat Corrales, a backup catcher behind Bench on Cincinnati's Big Red Machine.

When the Pirates edged the Braves 3–2 and 1–0 in the next two games, however, they took a 3–2 lead back home to Pittsburgh. Yet once again, Avery was pure poison for the Pirates. He matched Drabek through eight tense, scoreless innings. Olson's two-out double in the top of the ninth scored Ron Gant, and when Alejandro Peña struck out Van Slyke looking, Avery had his second 1–0 win over the Pirates.

I remember that at-bat clearly. It was one of those hold-your-breath moments. Peña threw him fastball after fastball, and Van Slyke hit line drive after line drive. But all of them landed just foul, including a couple in the seats.

It was a cold night, and on TV there was a shot of Avery sitting in the dugout with a ski mask covering half his face. After eight or nine pitches, Peña finally pulled the string and Van Slyke struck out looking at the only changeup Peña had thrown.

Avery had come up to the Braves in 1990 and, like many rookie pitchers, he struggled at first. He went 3–11 with a 5.64 ERA, but Bobby was not about to give up on him. And in 1991, Avery went 18–8 with a 3.38 ERA. He had become the pitcher the Braves always thought he could be.

Now in the postseason, Avery was proving he could pitch and win the big games. The first three full seasons he was with the team, from 1991–93, Avery went 47–25 and was as good as anybody. But then he started having arm trouble.

After the nine-inning drama of Game 6, Game 7 was a relative breeze. Brian Hunter hit a two-run home run in the first inning, and that was all Smoltz needed. He shut out the Pirates on four hits. Back home in Atlanta at the Fox Theatre that evening, during a performance of *The Phantom of the Opera*, many people in the audience listened to the game on the radio. The show's star, while taking his bows at the final curtain, held up four fingers—one for each run in the Braves' 4–0 lead.

When the game ended that way, Olson leaped into Smoltz's arms once again. In the clubhouse, Avery was sprayed with champagne while holding the NLCS Most Valuable Player award, and he tossed back his head, opened his mouth, and stuck out his tongue to drink the bubbly. He'd just set an NLCS record with 16⅓ scoreless innings.

Now we were on our way to Minneapolis.

It's still difficult to describe the emotion of that night. It was hard to believe: We were going to the World Series! The Atlanta Braves!

On the Delta charter to Minneapolis, reliever Marvin Freeman rapped while dancing in the aisle with, of all people, John Schuerholz. Marvin even took a joyride in the L-1011's cargo elevator that delivered meals to the flight attendants.

For the previous two months, the most commonly asked question whenever you boarded a team charter was, "How did the Dodgers do?" On this night, this flight, as I was walking up the aisle, third-base coach Jimy Williams stopped me. "I have a question for you," he said. "How did the Dodgers do?"

We both burst out laughing.

Our plane finally landed in Minneapolis at about 4:00 AM. We got to the Crown Sterling Hotel downtown around 5:00. When I awoke at 10:00 AM and pulled back the curtain in my room, I looked out the window and there it was—the Metrodome, just a couple of blocks away.

Yes, we were really here. I called Elaine and when she answered, I said, "Hi, this is Pete Van Wieren of the Atlanta Braves and"—in a much louder voice—"I'm at the World Series!"

Prior to the start of Game 1, the World Series party was held at the LaSalle Plaza on Friday night. I had attended functions like this before as traveling secretary to distribute tickets and credentials. But this time, we were the show. This time, executives from other teams were coming up and congratulating us. It was such a proud feeling.

The World Series began the next night, and what a memorable one it turned out to be. Two worst-to-first teams. Tomahawks versus homer hankies. As evenly matched a Series as you could ever ask for. By the time it got to Game 7 back in Minneapolis, the respect these teams had for each other was obvious.

The Twins won the first two games in the Metrodome, and then the World Series came to Atlanta for the first time. After flying home, I remember riding a bus from the airport carrying some National League executives to downtown. Sitting behind me was Jay Horwitz, the New York Mets vice president of media relations. He couldn't quite believe where we were either.

In his New York accent, Jay said, "This seems so bizarre to be coming to a World Series in At-lan-ta." I sat there laughing and thinking, "*It does seem bizarre. But it sure is fun.*"

No one had more fun in Atlanta than Mark Lemke. The little second baseman batted only .234 during the season, but in the World Series he took over. Lemke singled in the game-winning run in Game 3. He scored the winning run in Game 4 on pinch-hitter Jerry Willard's sacrifice fly in the bottom of the ninth. Then he tripled twice in a 14–5 victory in Game 5 to give the Braves a 3–2 lead in the series and prompt this headline in the *Journal-Constitution*: "Re-MARK-able!"

"The original dirt player," Bobby Cox admiringly called him.

Back in Minneapolis on Saturday night, with a chance to win the franchise's first World Championship since 1957, the Braves battled the Twins through 12 dramatic innings in Game 6. In the bottom of the twelfth, Bobby brought in Charlie Leibrandt for a rare relief appearance. Charlie hadn't pitched since starting and losing Game 1; he was making his first relief appearance since 1989.

It was a brief one. On a 2–1 count to the leadoff batter, Leibrandt left a changeup up and over the plate. Kirby Puckett drilled it into the left-field stands and forced a seventh and deciding game.

With Game 6 finally over, three busloads of Braves personnel left the Metrodome and headed out to the Radisson Inn in suburban Plymouth.

We had to switch hotels because a convention had booked all the downtown hotels in advance. We didn't arrive at the Radisson until nearly 1:00 AM, and a bunch of us headed straight toward the hotel bar.

They had just one girl working it.

"I'm sorry, folks," she said. "I've just given last call."

John Schuerholz, to his credit, walked up, introduced himself, and told her who we were. She called her manager, and he said, "Okay, we have to close soon. I'll take one drink order from each person."

Phil Niekro, who had managed at Triple A Richmond that season and was along for the trip, ordered first. He pointed and said, "I'll take that bottle of Crown Royal."

"The whole bottle, sir?"

"Yes."

Everyone was so wired; no one was ready to go to sleep. So everyone followed Knucksie's lead: "I'll take six beers…I'll take a bottle of Scotch." I don't know what their total take was, but it was a lot.

That was one of many memories from that night.

We all then proceeded to several rooms to wind down.

Then Sunday dawned, and evening finally arrived, bringing with it the seventh game of the greatest World Series ever.

That's the only World Series I've ever seen a hitter shake hands with a catcher before Game 7. Lonnie Smith walked up to the plate, stepped in to lead off the game, turned and shook hands with the Twins' Brian Harper. When have you ever seen that before?

That's the only World Series I've ever seen a player—Kent Hrbek of Minnesota—say in an interview before Game 7, "They ought to just cut the championship trophy in half and give it to each team."

That's the only World Series I've ever seen several players on a losing team—most notably Terry Pendleton—stay on the field and go over and shake the hands of the Twins, the winners. Just like after Game 7 of the Stanley Cup finals.

From the first pitch, it was clear that Game 7 was going to be a magnificent pitchers' duel between Minnesota's Jack Morris, the Game 1 winner, and John Smoltz, who'd gone 12–2 after the All-Star break before beating Pittsburgh twice in the NLCS. Through seven innings in the Metrodome, it was scoreless.

In the eighth, Lonnie Smith led off with a checked-swing single. He was running when Pendleton drilled a hit into the left-center field gap. But Smith hesitated as he neared second base. Perhaps he couldn't see the ball with all the white homer hankies Twins fans were waving in the dome. Or maybe Lonnie was deked by Twins rookie second baseman Chuck Knoblauch.

Whatever the reason, once Smith sped up, he could only reach third base. He was stranded there when, after Kent Hrbek fielded a force out at first base and David Justice was intentionally walked, Sid Bream bounced into a killing 3-2-3, first-to-home-to-first double play.

Lonnie's gaffe proved costly. In the tenth, after Smoltz had departed but Morris continued to shut down the Braves, Dan Gladden led off with a double and eventually scored on a bases-loaded pinch-single by Greg Olson's hunting buddy, Gene Larkin.

Minnesota 1, Atlanta 0. It was over.

I had the radio call of that tenth inning. In an effort to sum up the incredible year, I ended the broadcast by saying:

"The Minnesota Twins have won the World Series and may be the World Champions, but the Atlanta Braves have won the hearts of baseball fans all over America."

Steve Rushin of *Sports Illustrated* wrote, "Let us call this Series what it is, now, while its seven games still ring in our ears: the greatest that was ever played."

Furman Bisher may have summed it up best the next day in a column in the *Atlanta Journal-Constitution*: "The Atlanta Braves are the World Champions of outdoor baseball; the Minnesota Twins the indoor champions."

* * *

The highlights from that season are forever embedded in my memory:
- Terry Pendleton's National League Most Valuable Player year, and also his NL batting title with a .319 average. Tom Glavine's National League Cy Young Award, his first of two in the 1990s. Otis Nixon's club-record 72 stolen bases. Ron Gant's second straight 30–30 season, joining Willie Mays and Bobby Bonds as the only the third player to record 30 home runs and 30 steals in consecutive seasons. Bobby Cox, the National League Manager of the Year.
- A rainout on Opening Day. Sid Bream's grand slam on May 17 to beat his former team, the Pirates, 9–3. This, just after a three-game series in Chicago where three generations of Carays called those Braves-Cubs games: Harry, Skip, and young Chip. A small earthquake in Los Angeles in early July, when the Braves dropped two of three to the Dodgers and fell below .500 for the first time since May 1.
- Glavine's first nod as the National League's starting pitcher in the All-Star Game; Glav was also the club's first 20-game winner since Phil Niekro in 1979. Smoltz, focusing on Jack's Llewellyn's red shirt and making the opposition see red while winning six of his first seven starts after the break. Rally Caps, in four styles, courtesy of reliever Mark Grant.
- Los Angeles manager Tommy Lasorda doing popular TV commercials for his diet—and one of nearly 150 banners at that crucial mid-September series with the Dodgers, which parodied Lasorda's diet pitch: "I lost 9½ games in only nine weeks. And I owe it all to the Braves plan."
- The combined no-hitter thrown by Kent Mercker, Mark Wohlers, and Alejandro Peña—the first combined no-hitter in National League history.

Otis Nixon, after catching the final out, absentmindedly tossing the ball into the stands before realizing what he'd done and retrieving it for posterity. The closer's mentality inscription Peña wrote on the ball:

9-11-91
ATL-1, SD-0
Save #8

- Ted and Jane, of course. Ted Turner and Jane Fonda, in the owner's box throughout the postseason in their Braves caps and jackets, chopping and chanting along with everyone else—except when Ted nodded off from time to time. Ted and Jane's occasional guests, including Hank Aaron and former President Jimmy Carter and his wife, Rosalynn. They chopped, too.
- The Game 1 "Hefty Tag"—Kent Hrbek literally lifting Ron Gant up and off of first base to tag him and getting away with it when Gant was called out. Lonnie Smith homering in all three Series games in Atlanta. Lemke's World Series heroics. Lemmer hit .417 in the Series, including three triples. After Game 7, when an official from the Baseball Hall of Fame asked for one of Lemke's bats to take to Cooperstown, Mark—a native of Utica, New York—hesitated but agreed, saying, "The Hall of Fame is only 45 minutes from my home, so I can go visit it."
- And then, of course, there was the parade.

Two days after the World Series ended, a parade down Peachtree Street was scheduled as a salute to this remarkable, never-to-be-forgotten team. None of us were prepared for the turnout. Skip, Don, and I were assigned to ride together in one of the convertibles. As we slowly made our way down Peachtree Street, Atlanta's most famous thoroughfare, we were astounded by the sea of faces at every turn.

An estimated 750,000 fans turned out—lining every street, looking out every office building window, perched on lampposts, standing on cars. All of them cheering and chopping in appreciation of a remarkable season. It took a couple of hours for the motorcade to weave its way through the throngs on the route to City Hall. There, several thousand more fans were gathered and cheering.

At City Hall, John Schuerholz told the crowd, "There is no feeling in the world like this...nothing, no way. It has to be one of baseball's all-time great stories."

I am often asked, "What would it have been like if the Braves had won that World Series?"

My answer is always the same: "I can't imagine it being any better than it was. We weren't treated like we lost. It could not have been any better."

Chapter **8**

We Need a Fireman

When spring training began in 1992, the atmosphere was completely different. This was the Atlanta Braves, the defending National League champion. The crowds were larger everywhere we went, and so was the media coverage. Most were asking the same question, "Can the Braves do it again?"

While we felt good about our chances of repeating, nobody actually knew. The 1991 season had been such a wonderful storybook season and had happened so unexpectedly, it made everyone wonder: was it a once-in-a-lifetime kind of season?

During the final weeks of the 1991 season, I made it a point to walk around the club level at Atlanta-Fulton County Stadium any day that the Braves were at home to soak up the atmosphere, witness the fan's excitement, and savor the experience—just in case it never happened again.

Joe Simpson joined Skip, Don, and me after five years as a broadcaster for the Seattle Mariners. Like Don, Joe was a former Dodger who made his major league debut as a pinch-hitter for…Don Sutton.

Simpson finished his playing career with the Kansas City Royals, where he is best remembered for being the guy who held back George Brett during the famous "Pine Tar" incident in Yankee Stadium. When you see the clip, you'll easily spot Joe grabbing hold of George as he charged home-plate umpire Tim

McClelland. But what you don't hear is one of the other umpires asking Joe, "Have you got him?"

Joe Simpson got into broadcasting after being released by Kansas City general manager…John Schuerholz. So he had ties to our group before he even arrived. Joe's personality, sense of humor, and demeanor blended immediately with our style and format.

When the season began, we were hopeful that the second-half magic of 1991 would carry over, but it didn't start out well. By late May, the Braves were 20–27 and once again back in all-too-familiar territory—last place in the National League West.

But then came the turnaround, as close to a 180-degree about-face as possible. The Braves went 41–15 over the next 56 games and by late July had moved back into first place in the division. They won the NL West by a comfortable eight games and were headed for another National League Championship Series showdown with Barry Bonds and the Pittsburgh Pirates.

Bonds was the National League Most Valuable Player that season and, while he had not yet become the bulked-up Barry, he was already one of the game's great all-around players. He almost became a Brave in spring training. The Braves and Pirates had agreed to a deal, but Pittsburgh general manager Ted Simmons had to back out at the last minute because he couldn't get approval from his ownership.

In the hotel elevator that morning in West Palm Beach, John Schuerholz got on and said to me, "This will be a memorable day for the Braves."

I didn't know what he meant, and when nothing happened, I asked him about it later that day. That's when we found out how close we came to getting Barry Bonds. He was in the final year of his contract, and the Pirates knew this might be their last shot at getting to the World Series for a while. In fact, they haven't had a winning season since.

That season, the Braves were once again led by the trio of Terry Pendleton, David Justice, and Tom Glavine. Pendleton, coming off his National League MVP performance, put up MVP-caliber numbers again and batted .311 with 21 home runs and 105 RBIs. Meanwhile, Justice belted 21 homers and Glavine nearly matched his '91 NL Cy Young statistics with a 20–8 record and a 2.76

earned-run average. Yet not even Pendleton approached Bonds, who was voted the 1992 NL MVP in a landslide with a performance showcasing speed and power, batting and fielding. Bonds, too, batted .311, belted 34 homers, drove in 103 runs, stole 39 bases, and won another Gold Glove.

The two teams were pretty much the same as the previous year. The Pirates had added a knuckleballer, Tim Wakefield, who wound up winning two games in the NLCS. After the Braves took the first two games in Atlanta, Wakefield out-dueled Tom Glavine, 3–2, in Game 3 at Three Rivers Stadium. In Game 4, opening-game winner John Smoltz won again, beating Doug Drabek for the second time.

With Atlanta now holding a commanding 3–1 lead in the NLCS, it was an ex-Brave, Bob Walk, who pitched the game of his life in Game 5. Staked to a four-run lead in the first inning, Walk pitched a three-hitter and sent the series back to Atlanta.

In Game 6, it was Wakefield once again. The Braves had brought minor league pitching coach and former knuckleballer Bruce Dal Canton to throw batting practice. But it didn't work. The Pirates jumped all over Glavine, scoring eight runs in the second inning. Wakefield's knuckler mystified the Braves again in a 13–4 rout.

So once again it came down to Game 7—this time in Atlanta, where for the longest time it looked like the season would come to a premature end. Trailing 2–0 in the bottom of the ninth inning, the Braves rallied for one of the most dramatic victories in baseball history.

For eight innings, Doug Drabek had shut out the Braves. Yet to start the ninth inning, Pirates manager Jim Leyland opted to bring in his closer, Stan Belinda, a sidearming right-hander.

Don and I had worked the first 4½ innings on radio and were back in the press lounge watching the game on television. As the Braves began to rally, the two of us went and stood in the back of the radio booth, where Skip and Joe were on the air, to watch the finish live. I know Don and I weren't there when Jose Lind, the Pirates second baseman, committed a rare error. But I know we were there when pinch-hitter Francisco Cabrera came to the plate with two outs and the bases loaded.

Cabrera had delivered a huge home run in Cincinnati during the '91 pennant race, but he had bounced back and forth between Atlanta and its Richmond affiliate since then. He was a very good hitter who was about to deliver the biggest hit of his life.

Cabrera's line-drive base hit to left field scored David Justice and Sid Bream, and was called to perfection by Skip:

"Two balls, one strike… What tension. A lot of room in right-center. If he hits one there, we can dance in the streets. The 2–1…line drive left field! One run is in! Here comes Bream, here's the throw to the plate! He iiiiiiiiiiisss…………..safe! Braves win! Braves win! Braves win! Braves win!"

Pause.

"Braves win!!!"

The rest of Skip's call:

"They may have to hospitalize Sid Bream! He's down at the bottom of a huge pile at the plate. They help him to his feet. Frank Cabrera got the game-winner. The Atlanta Braves are National League champions again! This crowd is going berserk!"

And so were we. We were on our way to another World Series, this time against the Toronto Blue Jays.

I'll never forget that sequence: Cabrera hit the line drive. Justice scored easily. Sid Bream lumbered around third base with Justice signaling frantically for him to slide. Bonds uncorked the throw, Sid slid, and Randy Marsh signaled "Safe!" The Braves were in a huge pile at home plate, and the Pirates were in a state of shock. Bonds was down on one knee. Andy Van Slyke sat in disbelief in center field.

Marsh wasn't even scheduled to work the plate in Game 7. But when plate umpire John McSherry became ill early in the game and had to leave the field, Marsh moved behind the plate.

The following season, Marsh told us that just like players, umpires have big moments, too. And that was the biggest in his career. "All you want to do," he said, "is get it right."

Driving home after that unbelievable finish, I decided to stay off the Interstates—which would be clogged bumper-to-bumper with post-game traffic—and drive through downtown. I'm glad I did.

It was like New Year's Eve in Times Square. Horns were beeping; fans were high-fiving and hugging complete strangers. You could hear the chant echoing from the many taverns and clubs in Buckhead. All this in celebration of another Braves pennant.

The World Series opened in Atlanta with the Braves and Blue Jays splitting the first two games. Before Game 1, there was a major *faux pas*. A color guard marched onto the field near home plate, carrying the American and Canadian flags before the playing of both national anthems. There was one slight problem:

The red-and-white Canadian flag was being presented upside down, with the red maple leaf pointing down. It caused something of an uproar in Canada. When the Series shifted to Toronto, there were T-shirts on sale all over town that read:

1992 World Series
Toronto Blue Jays
Vs.
sǝʌɐɹ𝖡 ɐ𝗍uɐl𝗍∀

That's right, "Atlanta Braves" was printed upside down.

In Toronto before Game 3, Joe Simpson and I decided to go out to the Skydome early with our radio producer, Rick Shaw. We hailed a cab in front of the Sheraton Hotel and set out for the ballpark.

At the first intersection, we stopped for a red light. When the light changed, we proceeded through the intersection, but a car coming from our right ran the red light and slammed broadside into our cab. Rick, who was sitting in the rear passenger seat, took the brunt of the blow and was thrown across the seat into me, knocking my glasses off and ramming my head into the window.

We were both shaken up, but fortunately neither one was seriously hurt. Joe, who was riding in the front seat of the taxi, was okay. A TV news crew from

Atlanta, up to cover the Series, saw the accident and quickly came over to see if we were all right. Then they drove us to the ballpark, where Rick and I headed for the trainer's room in the Braves clubhouse—Rick to have his back looked at, and me to find a glasses repair kit.

While we were sitting there, Sean McDonough and Tim McCarver of CBS passed by on their way to their pregame meeting with Bobby Cox. Tim glanced into the trainer's room and did a double-take when he saw us.

We laughed and told him, "Just getting a rubdown before the big game."

The Series wound up going six games, with the Blue Jays winning 4–2 to become the first franchise from a foreign country to win a World Series. In three of their four victories, the Blue Jays victimized the Braves' bullpen.

In Game 1, Damon Berryhill's three-run homer in the sixth inning off our old nemesis Jack Morris gave Atlanta a 3–1 win. In Game 2, Jeff Reardon came on in the ninth inning with the Braves leading 4–3. The Braves closer, who had been acquired from the Red Sox on August 30, gave up a two-run home run to Toronto's Ed Sprague that beat the Braves, 5–4, and evened the Series at a game apiece.

Since Ernie Johnson had retired after the 1989 season and missed out on all the fun in '91, we invited him to take part in the radio broadcast of Game 2 of the '92 World Series. Ernie was on the air when Sprague homered and told us afterward, "I hope I didn't jinx you guys." He was so distraught; he really felt bad.

Up in Toronto, Game 3 in the Skydome was a repeat for Reardon. This time in the ninth inning he allowed a game-winning single to Candy Maldonado to give the Blue Jays a 3–2 victory and an advantage they never relinquished. Game 4 was another close loss, 2–1. All four Toronto victories were one-run games.

After Lonnie Smith's Game 5 grand slam kept the Braves' hopes alive with a 7–2 win, the Series returned to Atlanta-Fulton County Stadium.

In the ninth inning of Game 6, Otis Nixon's single tied the game at 3–3. But for the second straight World Series, veteran Charlie Leibrandt made a rare eleventh inning relief appearance that backfired.

This time, Leibrandt gave up a two-out double to Dave Winfield that gave Toronto a 4–2 lead. In the bottom of the eleventh, the Braves rallied for one run only to see Nixon try to drag-bunt his way on with a runner on base. When he was thrown out by reliever Mike Timlin, the Blue Jays rejoiced and celebrated the first of what would be two straight World Championships.

Although the Braves had won back-to-back National League pennants (something the franchise hadn't accomplished since 1957–58 while in Milwaukee), finding that reliable closer was proving elusive. While the starting rotation was terrific (and about to get even better), the 1991 and '92 seasons saw Atlanta use Juan Berenguer, Mike Stanton, Kent Mercker, Marvin Freeman, Jim Clancy, Jeff Parrett, Mark Wohlers, Alejandro Peña, and Armando Reynoso as the closer at various times.

If the Braves were going to continue this run of titles, they were going to have to find a more reliable fireman.

Before the 1993 season even began, the Braves significantly improved what was already the best young starting rotation in baseball.

Christmas arrived early that year for Atlanta. On December 9, the Braves signed free agent Greg Maddux to a lucrative five-year, multi-million-dollar contract. Maddux, who was only 26 years old, had just won his first NL Cy Young Award with the Chicago Cubs. He would go on to win the next three with the Atlanta Braves, a run of four consecutive Cy Young Awards still unequaled and one that may never be matched.

As the season progressed, it became evident that the Braves needed one more big bat if they were going to win a third straight division title. That big bat was acquired on July 18 when the Braves sent a trio of minor leaguers to San Diego in return for slugging first baseman Fred McGriff.

McGriff was scheduled to make his Atlanta debut on July 20 in a night game against the St. Louis Cardinals. A welcoming press conference was scheduled for 4:00 PM in the press lounge at Atlanta-Fulton County Stadium.

Shortly after 4:00, we were informed that McGriff was running late. The press conference—if there was time for one—would instead be held in the Braves' clubhouse. Skip and I returned to the radio booth and were talking about the season.

The Braves were playing good baseball with a record of 54–41. But the San Francisco Giants were playing *great* baseball. Their 63–32 record gave them a nine-game lead over Atlanta.

Maddux had joined an already strong starting rotation. Although he was leading the league in ERA, his record was just 9–7. The Braves just needed to provide more run support for Maddux, Glavine, Smoltz, and Avery—and McGriff seemed to be the answer.

Shortly before 6:00—first pitch was at 7:40—Skip and I were talking in the radio booth when we noticed some wisps of smoke coming from the radio sponsor's hospitality booth, three booths to our left. This wasn't unusual. The booth was catered for every game and the set-up was almost always in place a couple of hours before game time with hot *hors d'oeuvres* kept that way by Sterno burners.

But after awhile, the smoke thickened and smelled more like something was burning. We walked down the hall and tried to look inside. But the door was locked, so stadium maintenance was notified. When they arrived, they were unable to locate the correct key to unlock the door.

The smoke continued to grow even thicker, and now you could see flames through the glass dividers that separated the booths. Armed with a fire extinguisher, a maintenance man now began to walk along the front edge of the press level to get closer to the fire. To give him more room, Skip and I took our scorebooks into the press lounge to write down our lineups.

A few minutes later, our producer, Rick Shaw, rushed into the press lounge from the radio booth.

"Hey guys," Rick said, "you'd better come and get your stuff. That fire is only two booths away now."

Skip and I walked back into the booth, grabbed our briefcases, and decided to leave the press area altogether so that workers could deal with the fire. As we neared the exit door, nearly 50 yards away, there was a tremendous boom! Thick, black smoke came billowing through the press lounge. It was as if someone had turned on a power hose.

When we reached the concourse, we began trotting toward the press elevator.

"What the hell was that?" Skip asked.

"I don't know," I replied. "Let's just get out of here."

The press elevator had been turned off, so we walked down three levels of ramps and headed for the Braves clubhouse. When we got there, security guards were already getting everybody out onto the field. The stadium was being evacuated.

Once on the field, we couldn't believe what we were seeing. The radio booth that we had been sitting in ten minutes earlier was entirely engulfed in flames. So was most of the adjoining press box. Players, team officials, and media members milled around the outfield while firefighters arrived and began to battle the blaze.

Jeff Blauser and Mark Lemke, meanwhile, posed at home plate while holding their bats, their arms on each other's shoulders. Those two best buddies smiled broadly while Braves team photographer Walter Victor took their picture. Above Blauser and Lemmer, huge flames and black smoke billowed out of the booth.

It took nearly two hours before we were allowed back in the clubhouse. By then, the radio booth and press box were a blackened and charred total loss.

The fire apparently had started when a breeze blew part of a paper table-cloth into one of the Sterno burners. Once the flames reached the drop ceiling, which was shared by all of the booths on that level, the fire quickly spread. The boom that Skip and I heard was a steel beam above the drop ceiling exploding from the intense heat.

Thankfully, no one was injured. Amazingly, we played that night.

The game finally started about an hour-and-a-half late. Radio and television engineers jerry-rigged temporary broadcast facilities in a seating area on the club level just beyond the burned-out area. About 2,000 seats directly below the press box were also roped off and inaccessible to fans. And at 9:00 PM, the game between the Braves and Cardinals was finally underway.

Fred McGriff never did hold that press conference, at least not that night. But he did make his Braves debut a memorable one. "Crime Dog" hit a dramatic two-run homer that completed a five-run rally in the sixth inning. Shortly after midnight, the Braves finally beat St. Louis 8–5 to remain nine games behind the Giants.

"What a start," McGriff said afterward. When asked if he always made such dramatic entrances, Fred grinned and said, "With a bang." His arrival had literally fired up the Braves.

Atlanta went 50–17 the rest of the way, finally catching the Giants on September 10. The Braves wound up winning the National League West by one game in one of the greatest pennant races in baseball history.

Down the stretch during the last three weeks of the season, the Braves went 14–6, and the Giants went 14–8. It seemed like whenever the Braves won, so did the Giants. Whenever Atlanta lost, so did San Francisco. The division wasn't decided until the final day of the season.

The Braves defeated the expansion Colorado Rockies, 5–3, then lingered at Atlanta-Fulton County Stadium. So did about 20,000 fans left over from the sellout crowd. It was shades of 1991 as everyone—Braves and fans—watched on the big screen in center field as the Dodgers again eliminated their archrivals from San Francisco, 12–1.

During another raucous clubhouse celebration, I spotted shortstop Rafael Belliard and, shaking his hand, I said, "Three in a row, Raffy, three in a row!"

He looked back at me with a sly grin. "Four for me!" said Raffy, who had been a member of the 1990 NL East Division champion Pirates before joining the Braves in '91.

What a race '93 had been. The Braves finished with a record of 104–58, the Giants 103–59. Now it was on to a third straight NLCS, this time with the Philadelphia Phillies.

After losing the first game in Philadelphia, the Braves won a pair of lopsided victories, 14–3 and 9–4, to take a 2–1 lead in the series. And then the Braves simply seemed to run out of gas.

The nail-biting race with San Francisco had taken its toll. The Braves had little left in the tank. The Phillies swept the next three games and took the NLCS 4–2. Danny Jackson out-dueled John Smoltz 2–1 in Game 4. Lenny Dykstra hit a game-winning tenth-inning home run off Mark Wohlers in Game 5.

And in Game 6, a Mickey Morandini line drive hit Greg Maddux in the leg early in the game. Maddux remained in the game but clearly wasn't himself, as the Phillies won 6–3 to capture their first National League pennant since 1983.

Although there was no return trip to the World Series for a third straight year, the Braves garnered another Cy Young Award. Maddux went 20–10 and led the league with a 2.36 earned-run average to repeat as the NL Cy Young winner. Maddux and Tom Glavine—who went 22–6, with a 3.20 ERA—became the first Braves tandem to win 20 games in the same season since Warren Spahn and Lew Burdette did it with the Milwaukee Braves in 1959.

Add Smoltz (15–11, 3.62) and Steve Avery (18–6, 2.94) to Maddux and Glavine, and you had one of the best starting rotations in baseball history. The most common comparison to these four is the 1954 Cleveland Indians quartet of Bob Feller, Bob Lemon, Early Wynn, and Mike Garcia.

Three of those four—Feller, Lemon and Wynn—are in the Baseball Hall of Fame. And you know what? If all goes as expected, Maddux, Glavine, and Smoltz will join them there.

In addition to superb pitching, the foursome of Maddux, Glavine, Smoltz, and Avery became inseparable off the field. Whether it was a golf game on the days when they weren't pitching, a card game on the team charter, or just hanging around together, you hardly ever saw one of those pitchers without at least one or more of the others around him.

Despite their pitching excellence, the season had ended with that Game 6 loss in Philadelphia. After the game, a group of over-served Philly hooligans tried to tip over one of our team buses as it waited outside the Braves clubhouse. They failed.

But then the following year, the entire game of baseball tipped over on its own.

Chapter **9**

A Season Lost
an Answer Found

When the 1994 season began, we knew that a players' strike was not only possible but probable. The season started with an expired basic agreement between players and owners, and talks were going nowhere. The owners wanted a salary cap, the players didn't, and neither side seemed willing to compromise.

The Braves opened the season in mid-season form, going 13–1 to equal the best start in franchise history. Yet there was a sense of, "Does it matter?" pervading anything that was happening on the field. By early August, talks between the players and owners had broken down.

The Braves flew home from Colorado after a 13–0 win on August 11 knowing that the strike was set to begin on the following day. None of us had any inkling that it would last as long as it did.

There had been strikes and lockouts before, one of which lasted two months in 1981. But there had always been a resolution in time for the regular season to conclude and a full postseason to commence. Not this time.

It was agonizing watching millionaires and billionaires bicker over dollars. There was little sympathy for either side. When baseball commissioner Bud Selig announced the cancellation of the 1994 postseason, I was actually a little teary-eyed.

How could they do this to the game?

While all of this was going on, there was an unexpected revelation regarding my father. After learning the truth about him when I was a high school senior, there remained a natural curiosity over his whereabouts. I learned that I had another set of grandparents—and in 1963, I met them for the first time at their Buffalo, New York, home.

Joseph and Katherine Van Wieren seemed like wonderful people. But they were unable to help when it came to finding Howard. They had not seen or heard from him in years, either. Unfortunately, after that meeting, I never saw or heard from my paternal grandparents again.

I wrote to them, inviting them to visit me at Cornell, but I received no answer. Years later, after both of them had died, we learned that they were both ashamed of what their son had done and fearful that we were seeking their financial help—which we were not.

Other than that visit, there was very little we could do to try to find Howard. At some point during my college years, we heard a rumor that he might be working for a circus. We contacted Ringling Brothers, Cole Brothers, and the Clyde Beatty companies, but none of them had a Howard Van Wieren in their employ.

It was a situation that was always in the back of my mind. Whenever I checked into a hotel on a road trip, one of the first things I would always do was check the telephone directory in my room just on the chance that a Howard or an H. Van Wieren might be listed.

None ever was.

Don't get me wrong. This was not an obsession of mine. Months, and even years, would go by when I would not think about it. But something would always come up that would remind me of it again. For example, when our telecasts began going nationwide on TBS via cable, my mother and I both wondered if some day Howard might see me on TV and I would get a call or a letter from him wondering if he was my father.

We needn't have worried. That never happened.

It certainly wasn't on my mind on that August day in 1994, while I was sitting at home because of the baseball strike. I received a call from my cousin,

My mother was a legal secretary. This image was taken four months after my birth in 1944.

Always a baseball fan, here I am in my catcher's gear in the summer of 1951.

Borrowing our name from the popular movie starring Paul Newman and Jackie Gleason, I played drums and sang with a band called The Hustlers while attending Cornell. Left to right: Carmine Lanciani, Chuck Goulding, me, Dave Karr, and Ric Holt.

When the broadcasting of the Binghamton Triplets minor-league games ceased in 1968, I picked up other jobs including hosting Challenge Bowling *every Sunday at noon with Joe Strano (right).*

A family photo from 1973: Pete, Elaine, Jon, and Steve.

My original broadcast team with the Atlanta Braves was (left to right) Skip Caray, Ernie Johnson, and me.

Ernie Johnson (right) and I in our ostrich racing silks in 1976. The pregame promotion was supposed to be a one-lap race around the stadium—until my ostrich decided to keep going.

The 1988 Atlanta Braves telecast team for SuperStation TBS was (left to right): me, Ernie Johnson, Billy Sample, and Skip Caray.

Riding with me in the 1991 parade on Peachtree Street in Atlanta were my broadcasting teammates Skip Caray and Don Sutton.

Atlanta Braves players Mark Lemke (left) and Jeff Blauser pose while the pressbox at Atlanta–Fulton County Stadium burned in July 1993.

The logo for "Skip and Pete's Hall of Fame Barbecue" at Turner Field.

In the dugout with Bobby Cox and Skip Caray on the day that the Braves honored Skip and me for our 25th year as Braves broadcasters.

Marsha Flagg, in Rochester. She had just returned from a Christian youth camp in upstate New York, where she'd served as a counselor.

While there, Marsha and some others were looking through photo albums of previous camps. They'd gotten to some old black-and-white photos taken in the early 1940s when she heard someone say, "That's Howard Van Wieren. He went to our church. And I think that is the girl he married."

Marsha looked at the photo more closely and, sure enough, "the girl" was her Aunt Ruth, my mother. Marsha asked the woman if she knew what had happened to Howard, and she was told that he had died 25 or 30 years ago. She wasn't sure exactly when, but she knew someone who would know.

Marsha wrote down the names and informed my mother, who then got in touch with Donald and Eileen Dykstra, who lived in Buffalo. Donald was Howard's cousin. The correspondence included letters and telephone calls. Little by little, we learned the answers to the questions we'd had for so long.

From Mrs. Dykstra's telephone conversation with my mother:

"Howard was picked up as a derelict on the street in New York City. After a few days, he died. It was somewhere around 1971. He was buried in New York's Potter's Field.

"There was no embalming or any kind of funeral. When people die under these circumstances, they merely place them in a pine box and bury them in the city's burial grounds. Howard's father, Joseph, was notified of his son's death but wanted nothing to do with him. He refused to go to New York to claim the body."

My mother then began the tedious process of trying to obtain a copy of the death certificate from the New York Bureau of Records and Statistics. This bureaucratic process took nearly two years.

Finally, one day in February 1996, I received a letter from my mother along with a copy of Howard's death certificate. The details, or lack of them, tell a stark story.

Date of death: January 11, 1971.

Place of death: Metropolitan Hospital, Manhattan.

Age: 54.

Length of residence in New York City: Life.

Marital status: Single.

Name of surviving spouse: None.

Usual occupation: None.

Funeral director: None.

There was also an address given, which I wrote down and tucked into my wallet.

My mother's accompanying note pretty well summed up both of our feelings.

"I know what you know about your father and his effect on our lives would certainly not incline you to have much feelings for him, one way or another. What he was doing during those years, how he lived, how long he had lived in New York and many other questions, we will never know. What we do know is that he didn't care anything about either one of us, me before you were born and both of us after you were born. But now, we know he is gone and after 52 years, he is finally out of our lives."

People who know the story have asked me what I would have done if he had suddenly showed up. I would have asked him, "Why? Why did he abandon his wife and son? Did he ever think about the damage his actions caused? Did he care?"

Then, I would have told him to go away and never come back. There never would have been a relationship.

After learning all of this, I decided to visit his grave just so I could look down and say, "Well, I finally found you." But this proved impossible. Potter's Field is on Hart Island, a few miles from Manhattan, and is inaccessible to the public. The burial grounds are manned by prisoners from Riker's Island, and the graves are unmarked. I also learned that the simple coffins are stacked five deep in numbered sections three rows by ten rows. It's just a dump, is what it is.

Knowing what I do about his life, this seems like an appropriate final resting place.

Despite this situation that hung over our lives for so many years, my mother and I were getting on with our lives. I had my dream job in baseball, and my mother had prospered as a secretary and office manager for high-profile lawyers and politicians.

But there was something missing in my mother's life. All that changed in 1969 when she remarried. Her new husband and my stepfather was a wonderful man, James Shannon, and their wedding made national headlines.

Up until 1968, Jim had been a Catholic priest and had risen to the rank of auxiliary bishop of the Minneapolis-St. Paul diocese. He resigned from the priesthood in 1968 due to his strong opposition to Pope Paul's encyclical of that same year.

On August 2, 1969, Jim and my mother were married in a small, private ceremony in the minister's study at the First Christian Church in Endicott, New York. Elaine and I served as matron of honor and best man in a service attended by a few members of our family.

At the time, Jim was the highest-ranking former priest to marry. Knowing that this would draw media attention, news of the wedding was to be withheld for one week. That would give Jim and my mother time to make the cross-country drive to Santa Fe, New Mexico, where Jim had landed a job as assistant to the president of St. John's College.

But a disgruntled cousin, who knew of the wedding plans but was not invited to the ceremony, leaked word to the *Rochester Democrat & Chronicle* a few days later. And all hell broke loose.

My mother and Jim were in transit and out of contact, but the media found me. For days, I was answering the telephone and talking to writers from the *New York Times, Washington Post, Minneapolis Star-Tribune, Time, Newsweek,* and dozens of other publications. I acknowledged that the wedding had taken place but told them little else.

Many of their questions had to do with my real father. In a *New York Times* article from August 11, 1969, I am quoted as saying, "I have never met the man, and I don't know if he is still alive." We know now that Howard was alive and living in New York. I wonder if he read the *Times* that day?

Things did not quiet down for quite awhile. A larger-than-ever number of clergy were leaving the Catholic Church. The February 23, 1970, issue of *Time* magazine featured a cover story titled "The Catholic Exodus: Why Priests and

Nuns are Quitting." Two portraits shared the cover: former nun Anita Caspary and James Shannon, my new stepfather.

Eventually, the furor calmed, and Jim and my mother had a long and happy life together. A brilliant man—he received a doctorate in history from Yale University in 1954—Jim enrolled in law school in New Mexico. At age 48, he got his law degree and eventually moved back to Minneapolis, where he served as executive director of the Minneapolis Foundation. Jim moved on to become executive director of the General Mills Foundation and, upon retirement, served as a consultant for the Council on Foundations in Washington. He died in 2003.

During their 34 years together, Jim and my mother traveled the world. They had a wonderful life. After the heartbreak my mother suffered with Howard, she deserved it.

Chapter 10

From the Surreal to the Sublime

As spring training approached in 1995, there had been no resolution to the players' strike. But Major League Baseball was determined to have a season, so camps opened in February with so-called "replacement players."

When you walked into the Braves clubhouse that spring, you were greeted by a strange sight. There were the players wearing Braves uniforms, but who were these guys? Only a couple of the faces were familiar: Jose Alvarez and Marty Clary had pitched for Atlanta in the late 1980s, and outfielder Terry Blocker had been a Brave in 1988 and '89.

But the rest were a collection of never-weres and wannabes who had come from all over to play the part of a major league ballplayer. Most of them had some professional experience, but for many of them, that experience was at the Independent League level. Just figuring out who was who took days.

Outwardly, it looked much like any other spring training camp. But inside, there were major differences. There was no sense of camaraderie—we didn't know the players, and they didn't know each other. There was also a general sense of uneasiness among players, coaches, and executives.

No one knew how long this would last. It might be a week…it might be a year. But when the regular players came back, all of these replacements would be history. It reminded me of a fantasy camp.

Our radio broadcasts during that spring took on a different tone. Normally, we would focus on the one or two new additions to the team—which rookies had a chance to make it, who would win that final spot in the bullpen.

But that spring, we were introducing the fans to an entire roster of new-comers. The Braves had three right-handed pitchers named Brown at that 1994 camp. I'm not sure we ever knew for sure which one was which.

After a couple of weeks of games, Skip and I were in the Braves dugout one day prior to a game discussing the unusual spring with some Atlanta media members who had just arrived.

Skip was telling them, "The games are competitive. Everybody has the same talent pool—and after a couple of games, you kind of get to know these players."

"The fans will quickly choose their favorites," I added. "It'll be like the first year of an expansion team for everybody."

Third-base coach Jimy Williams was seated nearby and overheard our remarks.

"Pete, Skip," Jimy said in a disgusted tone. "This isn't Major League Baseball! This isn't Minor League Baseball! I don't know what this is—but it's awful!" And he got up and walked away.

Skip and I looked at each other. Jimy was right. Who were we kidding? As happy as we were to have baseball back and to be working again, the games presented were a sham.

The fans weren't buying into it, either. Instead of our usual West Palm Beach crowds of better than 5,000, these games were only drawing 1,000 or so. We needed the regular players to return.

As this replacement-player spring training entered its final week, an unbelievable tragedy occurred. On the evening of March 24, pitcher Dave Shotkoski went for his usual after-dinner stroll outside our hotel. He had gotten only about 500 yards away when a man on a bicycle rode up to him, pulled out a gun, and asked for his money.

When Shotkoski resisted, the man fired the pistol, killing the 30-year-old Chicago native who had spent six years in the minor leagues, two of them in the Braves organization.

The next day was so bizarre. A lot of players found out about Dave as they arrived at the ballpark. All baseball activities were canceled by the Braves. Municipal Stadium instead became the backdrop for a news conference outside the PR office that was conducted by stunned Braves officials and representatives from the West Palm Beach police department. The two people taking questions were John Schuerholz and a homicide detective.

Witnesses had given a good description of the suspect. What happened next could have come straight from a Hollywood script. Terry Blocker, the one-time Brave, had struck up a friendship with Shotkoski when they were assigned adjoining lockers in the Braves clubhouse. When he heard the news, Blocker decided to take action.

He called a couple of acquaintances from previous springs in West Palm Beach and had them take him into one of the city's toughest neighborhoods, where he started asking questions.

"A couple of times I felt I was in danger," Blocker told *New York Times* columnist George Vecsey, "but I was at peace with myself."

Blocker came up empty the first night, but he went back the next day and was able to learn the identity of the shooter. "All I had was his street name," Blocker said. But that was enough for police. They quickly made an arrest, charging the 29-year-old—who had a long arrest record—with first-degree murder.

Blocker was hailed as a hero by the police and the media.

"It was totally different from anything I've done in my life," Blocker told Vecsey. "After I came back to myself, I asked myself, 'Man, what was I thinking about?' But, I fear no man—I fear only God, and this was His will."

That dramatic and incredibly sad episode hung over the final week of spring training like a dark cloud. At the end of that week, the replacement Braves flew to Atlanta for their final two preseason games.

Once again, the fans stayed away. These final two games of the spring have become a tradition in Atlanta. They normally draw about 30,000 fans anxious for a sneak preview of the team. But the 1995 exhibition games drew only about 4,000 apiece.

At the end of the final preseason game, the replacement players who had survived the six-week tryout camp were expecting to receive an itinerary for the upcoming trip to San Diego, where the Braves were scheduled to open the season two days later. Instead, they each received a check for $1,000 and their walking papers.

The strike was over. The regular players were coming back. The start of the regular season was pushed back three weeks. And instead of San Diego, we headed back to West Palm Beach for more spring training. The atmosphere was dramatically different. Familiar faces were once again wearing Braves uniforms. The clubhouse was loose. It was back to business as usual after seven depressing months.

Anyone in baseball will tell you that spring training is one of their favorite times of the year. Everybody is undefeated and optimistic.

The atmosphere is casual and relaxed. And, of course, you can't beat the weather.

When the Braves trained in West Palm Beach, they had a table at the Palm Beach Kennel Club. This became a nightly gathering place for a rotating cast of players, coaches, minor-league managers, front office personnel, and members of the media. It gave us an opportunity to get to know each other better, have some laughs, and maybe win a couple of bucks.

A favorite spring training routine of mine was lunch with the major league scouts in the stadium pressrooms prior to games. There were always tales of players, coaches, managers, and teams past and present.

One of my favorite exchanges occurred one spring in West Palm Beach in the TeePee Room at Municipal Stadium. Scouts were quizzing each other on who was the best defensive third baseman they had ever seen.

"It has to be Brooks Robinson," said Hugh Alexander, the venerable scout for the Cubs. Others at the table were nodding their heads in agreement.

Then the Cardinals' Tim Thompson put in a plug for one of his own.

"I agree, Brooks was great," Thompson said. "But if you watched the Cardinals play every day back in the sixties, I don't know if you could have played the position any better than Ken Boyer did."

"Ken Boyer!" the Giants' Buddy Kerr scoffed. "He wasn't even the best fielding third baseman in his family!" The table erupted in laughter. Buddy had a point. Clete was pretty good.

Not all spring training memories were good ones. In 1978, when I was still doubling as traveling secretary, Ernie Johnson and I were in the radio booth at Municipal Stadium, just minutes from taking the air.

In walked a very upset Buzz Capra. The right-handed pitcher had led the National League in ERA in 1974, but he blew out his shoulder the following season. After surgery, he was never the same. Capra had just been given his release by the Braves and was in tears.

I had to leave the booth, return to my office, and make arrangements for Buzz to fly home to Illinois. It was hard seeing such a popular and likeable guy experiencing the end of his playing career. But these kinds of stories happen every spring.

On the flip side, there are those happy moments when a player who didn't expect to make the team finds out that he has. Rick Camp in 1976. Greg McMichael in 1993. And a host of others. Remembering Ernie's phone call to me in 1975, I knew exactly how they felt.

Occasionally, something truly bizarre occurred. The stadium in West Palm Beach was located next to the West Palm Beach Auditorium, which hosted all kinds of events. One spring, a rodeo was taking place when a Brahma bull that was tethered in a holding area outside broke loose.

While Braves equipment manager John Holland was sitting outside the clubhouse waiting for the team bus to return from a road trip, the bull came trotting by with a couple of men on horseback in pursuit. The bull panicked after being cornered and crashed through the plate-glass front of the Braves minor league office and clubhouse complex, causing more than a little damage. It took days to clean up and repair the building.

It was going to take much longer to clean up and repair Major League Baseball after the damaging strike. But the return of the regular players was an important first step.

At last, the 1995 regular season started on April 26. The crowd in Atlanta-Fulton County Stadium was smaller than usual for an opener—just a little more than 32,000—but this was true all over Major League Baseball because of the strike. The Braves beat the San Francisco Giants 12–5. Fred McGriff hit two home runs and drove in five runs.

I remember saying at some point during the broadcast, "If the Braves play like this all year, the fans will be back."

After six weeks, Atlanta was 20–17, in third place, and 4½ games behind the Phillies. But then the Braves turned it on. Once that happened, there was no looking back. The Braves went 70–37 the rest of the way, moved into first place on July 4, clinched the division crown on September 13, and easily won the NL East by 21 games over both the Phillies and the Mets.

Greg Maddux captured his fourth consecutive Cy Young Award, going 19–2 with a 1.63 ERA. He became the first pitcher to post back-to-back ERAs under 2.00 since Walter Johnson in 1918–19.

The offense was anchored by McGriff. "Crime Dog" hit 27 home runs and drove in 93 runs. An influx of terrific young talent provided more offensive punch. Catcher Javy Lopez (.315, 14 HR) and outfielder Ryan Klesko (.310, 23 HR) were in their second full seasons. Third baseman Chipper Jones (23 HR, 85 RBI) was the runner-up to Dodgers pitcher Hideo Nomo for National League Rookie of the Year.

My assignment for postseason play in 1995 was a little different. In 1994, Major League Baseball formed a partnership with ABC and NBC television, creating the Baseball Network. Every Monday night since then, Baseball Night in America had televised all of that evening's games on one of the networks, using a broadcaster from each team. I had been selected as the Braves representative.

In 1995, John Filipelli, executive producer of the telecasts, chose me as one of the postseason announcers. He told the *Atlanta Journal-Constitution*, "Pete has paid his dues. He deserves this chance. We also happen to believe that he is one of the best play-by-play announcers in the country."

I was proud and flattered to not only be chosen but to read those words. My assignment turned out to be the National League Division Series between the Braves and the Colorado Rockies. In the first year of the expanded playoff format—the Rockies were the NL Wild Card team—I would work alongside Larry Dierker, the Houston Astros broadcaster and future manager.

There was some concern about using one of the participating teams' broadcasters for a network telecast. But I tried to be as objective as I could and received no criticism after the broadcasts for being pro-Braves.

Larry and I clicked from the start. In Game 1, we were able to develop the point that Rockies manager Don Baylor was rolling the dice by using his final three position players off the bench in the seventh inning as Colorado attempted to take the lead. The rally fizzled, and with the Braves leading 5–4 in the ninth inning after Chipper's second homer of the game, it came down to this situation—bases loaded, two outs, and the pitcher due up for Colorado.

Baylor's gamble had backfired. He had to use pitcher Lance Painter as a pinch-hitter. Mark Wohlers struck him out, and the Braves were up 1–0 in the best-of-five series.

In Game 2, the ball was flying again in Coors Field in the rarefied air of the Mile High City. Marquis Grissom, who had homered in the opening game, hit two more home runs in Game 2. But it was a pair of RBI singles by McGriff and pinch-hitter Mike Mordecai that keyed Atlanta's four-run ninth-inning rally to give the Braves a 7–4 win and a 2–0 lead in the NLDS.

Back in Atlanta for Game 3, the Rockies avoided a sweep by belting two home runs en route to a 7–5 victory in 10 innings. But Game 4 was no contest, not even after Colorado scored three runs off Maddux in the third inning. The Braves immediately responded with four runs in the bottom half, then added six more over the next three innings and won easily, 10–4.

McGriff homered twice. Grissom went 5-for-5, setting a franchise record for base hits in a postseason game. The Braves, headed for a third straight National League Championship Series, looked exactly like who they were—the best team in baseball.

My Baseball Network assignment went very well. Working that series with Dierker established a friendship and mutual respect that exists to this day. We truly enjoyed the experience.

The next series with Cincinnati was no contest at all. The Braves easily swept the Reds, the first four-game sweep in NLCS history. While the first two games in Cincinnati went into extra innings, there was little doubt about the eventual outcome.

After Atlanta scored in the ninth inning of the opener to tie it 1–1, Mike Devereaux, the outfielder acquired from the Chicago White Sox in August, singled in the game-winning run in the eleventh. Devereaux would later be chosen the Most Valuable Player of the NLCS. In Game 2, the Braves broke a 2–2 tie in the tenth at Riverfront Stadium with four runs—the cushion arrived with Javy Lopez's three-run homer—to clinch a 6–2 victory.

Back home in Atlanta-Fulton County Stadium, the Braves dominated.

Maddux allowed just one run in eight innings of that 5–2 Game 3 victory. Chipper Jones had three hits, including a home run. Even catcher Charlie O'Brien supplied some rare power with a three-run homer. Game 4 was almost a foregone conclusion.

After a sub-par 7–13 season for him, Steve Avery started in a 6–0 shutout to lead Atlanta to a four-game sweep. Avery became the first pitcher in NLCS history to start three shutouts, adding to his two scoreless performances in 1991 against Pittsburgh. And Devereaux, playing in right field for David Justice, who was out with an injured knee, hit a three-run homer in the seventh inning. That ended any doubt about the outcome. It also clinched the MVP trophy for Devereaux, one of Atlanta's most timely and valuable late-season acquisitions ever.

The quartet of Glavine, Smoltz, Maddux, and Avery had completely shut down the Cincinnati lineup. In particular, outfielder Reggie Sanders, who had been a big run producer with 28 homers and 99 RBIs during the regular season. But in the NLCS, any time Cincinnati mounted a threat, it seemed that Sanders was the next hitter. For the series, he went 2-for-16, drove in no runs, and struck out 10 times.

It was on to another World Series—this time against the Cleveland Indians. While the Braves were winning their division by 21 games, Cleveland won the American League Central Division that year by an astounding 30 games over second-place Kansas City. The Series shaped up as a battle between Atlanta's superb starting pitching and the Indians' potent lineup, which featured the likes of Eddie Murray, Albert Belle, Jim Thome, Manny Ramirez, and speedster Kenny Lofton.

That season, the Indians led the American League in batting average (a collective .291), runs, base hits, and stolen bases. Cleveland had eight .300 hitters in its starting lineup. But the Braves had incomparable pitching.

Game 1 in Atlanta showcased Greg Maddux at his best. With only 95 pitches, Maddux limited the powerful Tribe to just a pair of singles—the fewest hits for Cleveland in a game all season—as the Braves won 3–2. It was a display of pitching, power, and precision by Atlanta. Fred McGriff homered in his first career World Series at-bat, and Rafael Belliard drove in a crucial run with a successful suicide squeeze bunt.

The next night, Tom Glavine was nearly as good as Maddux, allowing only three hits in a 4–3 Atlanta win. A two-run home run by Javy Lopez in the sixth inning gave Atlanta a 4–2 lead, and Glavine—with a save by Wohlers—made it stand up.

The following day we flew to Cleveland, where the Indians threw a huge party Monday night at the Rock and Roll Hall of Fame on the eve of Game 3. While we were there, a man came up to me and introduced himself. It was Ken Schanzer, executive vice president of NBC Sports, who complimented me on the work I had done in the Division Series for his network. Earlier in the day, I had received a call from Atlanta extending my contract for three more years. This was turning out to be a pretty good week. Now if only we could win the World Series.

It was extremely cold in Cleveland. The next morning, I accompanied my wife, Elaine, to a nearby department store, where she was going to look for a warm hat. We ran into umpire Harry Wendelstedt and his wife, who were there for the same reason. Harry and I sat back and, like *American Idol* judges, gave a thumbs up or thumbs down to each of the hats the girls tried on.

After the choices were made and we were leaving the store, Harry hung back and said to me, in a voice that our wives couldn't hear, "That was tougher than working the plate."

By game time, I was wishing I had bought a hat, too. It was 49 degrees, but a 25 mph wind off Lake Erie made it feel much, much colder in Jacobs Field. While John Smoltz lasted only 2⅓ innings, the game lasted four hours and nine minutes. It felt even longer. Finally, well after midnight, on an eleventh inning, game-winning single by Eddie Murray off of Alejandro Peña, the Indians prevailed 5–4.

As we tried to warm up in the Stadium Club after the game, all the talk was about Kenny Lofton. The Cleveland center fielder had reached base six times that night with two singles, a double, and three walks. Lofton had also already stolen five bases in the first three games.

We ran into Paul Snyder, whose work in scouting and player development over the years had contributed so heavily to the Braves' success.

"If we can get Lofton out, we'll win the Series," Snyder predicted.

Never were truer words spoken.

The next night, Lofton went 0-for-4 as the Braves defeated Cleveland, 5–2. Steve Avery got the win—the first, and unfortunately only, World Series victory of his career. When Wohlers faltered in the ninth inning, left-hander Pedro Borbón Jr. came on to strike out Jim Thome and Sandy Alomar, then he retired Lofton on a fly ball to right, ending the game and giving Atlanta a 3–1 lead in the series.

Pedro Borbón Sr. had been a mainstay in the Cincinnati Reds bullpen during the days of the Big Red Machine. Pedro Jr. always carried a picture from those days, taken at one of the Reds' father-and-son games. The kids in the photo included Pedro Jr., Pete Rose Jr., Eduardo Perez (son of Tony), and Ken Griffey Jr.—all future major leaguers.

The Indians avoided elimination in Game 5, scoring off Maddux early then holding on to win 5–4 and send the World Series back to Atlanta.

During the off-day workout in Atlanta on the eve of Game 6, David Justice took a verbal shot at Braves fans. "If we get down 1–0, they'll probably boo us out of the stadium," said the Braves outfielder. "Shoot! Up in Cleveland, they were down three runs in the ninth inning and they were still on their feet."

This critique outraged the Braves faithful. When Justice was introduced in Game 6, he was greeted with a lusty chorus of boos by a capacity crowd. The normally laid-back Atlanta fans responded to Justice's accusations with one of their more boisterous and animated performances ever. If Justice believed that Cleveland fans were louder, Braves fans that night were out to disprove him.

Tom Glavine turned in a masterful Game 6 performance. Midway through a scoreless game, walking back into the Braves dugout after one inning, Glavine shouted loudly—loud enough for all his teammates to hear:

"Just get me one run! That's all I need!"

That one run was provided in the bottom half of the sixth inning by—who else—David Justice. Turning on a Jim Poole fastball, Justice dramatically drove it into the right-field seats. As it turned out, that was all Glavine needed. Tom pitched eight innings of one-hit, shutout ball before Mark Wohlers came on in the ninth.

I worked the first half of Game 6 on Braves radio and was standing in the back of the radio booth when Skip delivered the call Braves fans had been waiting 30 years to hear:

"Mark into the wind. The 1–2 pitch, here it is…swung, popped up. Short left field, everybody's chasing it…Belliard's got it! In foul territory! Great play! One out.

"The 1–2 pitch, here it is…swung, fly ball, deep center. Grissom back…he's got room, plenty of room. Two out!

"Mark gets the sign. The wind and the pitch, here it is…Swung, fly ball, deep left-center. Grissom on the run…Yes! Yes! Yes! The Atlanta Braves have given you a championship! Listen to this crowd!

"A mob scene on the field! Wohlers gets 'em 1–2–3! A couple of fans rushing on the field.

"The Atlanta Braves have brought the first championship to Atlanta!"

It was not only the Braves' first-ever World Series title since moving to Atlanta in 1966. It was the city's first and only world championship by a franchise in a major professional sport.

Normally, after a postseason game, I would head straight to the postgame party tent. But on this night, I went down to the field to congratulate Bobby, his coaches, and players. When I saw Justice, he was beaming.

"Did you hear our fans tonight? Did you hear them?" he asked. "They were awesome!"

There were so many individual superlatives. Marquis Grissom had nine hits in the World Series, giving him 25 in the Braves' three October series—the most ever in a single postseason. He also hit safely in all 14 postseason games, the longest consecutive-game hitting streak in one postseason. Chipper Jones had 19 hits, the most ever by a rookie in the postseason. And Ryan Klesko became the first player ever to homer in three straight World Series road games.

Glavine, who allowed just one hit—Tony Peña's leadoff single in the sixth inning—and beat Cleveland twice, was named the World Series Most Valuable Player. He and the rest of the rotation and bullpen combined to hold the Indians to a .179 team batting average in the six-game series.

But most importantly, the Atlanta Braves had finally won the World Series. While capturing the franchise's third World Championship, the Braves became the first major league franchise to win world titles while based in three different cities: Boston in 1914, Milwaukee in 1957, and now Atlanta in 1995.

Two days later, we were part of another celebratory parade down Peachtree Street. To prevent individual cars from getting stalled by the crowd, they had us ride atop fire trucks. The turnout was tremendous, the joy was genuine, and the pride of the team and the city was on display for all to see. But there will never be a parade to top the 1991 parade.

Chapter *11*

The Rotten Apple

Whenever a team wins the World Series, the speculation begins almost immediately. Can they do it again? As the 1996 season approached, the Braves had every reason to believe they could. They had the best starting rotation in the game, a solid everyday lineup, and a farm system deep with prospects.

Spring training attracted more media attention than usual. This was no longer the quirky team that had a huge national following on cable TV but didn't win much. This was now, more than ever, "America's Team," the defending World Champions who had now played in three of the last four World Series. The opening of the 1996 season was anxiously anticipated.

But before the first pitch of the new season was thrown, the rewards for 1995 were due. The raising of the World Championship flag and the presentation of World Series Championship rings took place on Opening Day. As the field emcee of the event, I was able to witness up close and personal the pride of accomplishment as each player received his ring.

A World Series ring is baseball's Holy Grail. Anyone who has ever worn a major league uniform considers "the ring" the ultimate achievement in the game. But once the rings are awarded, you hardly ever see them being worn.

Their value, on both a personal and financial level, makes it too risky to take a chance on accidentally leaving it in a hotel room or in a clubhouse lock-box. Bobby Cox learned the hard way about treating such a prized possession casually.

In spring training of 1979, Bobby's second year as Braves manager, he was loading up his car at the stadium in West Palm Beach. While doing so, he took off his 1977 New York Yankees championship ring—he was a coach for that team—and placed it atop the car.

When Bobby was ready to depart, he forgot about the ring and started to drive away. Suddenly, Bobby remembered his prized possession and stopped the car, getting out to retrieve it. What he saw sickened him. The ring had fallen off and onto the pavement, and he had driven over it. What remained was a flattened chunk of precious metal and jewels.

Bobby later attempted to have it reshaped by a jeweler, but the result had only a vague resemblance to the original.

"From now on," he vowed, "any rings I receive will be locked up for safe-keeping."

Apparently, most players felt the same way. That was not the case with the broadcasters and executives, who also received a ring. But, of course, we didn't have to take them off to play a game. I wore mine proudly whenever I was at the ballpark.

If you want to see a player's ring, your best bet is to wait until the player retires. Then those rings tend to be worn more frequently, perhaps as a tangible reminder of the career highlight each ring represents. For example, Ernie Johnson frequently wore his 1957 Milwaukee Braves World Championship ring. And at any baseball alumni function, the variety of rings on display can be impressive.

Once the ceremonies were completed that Opening Day, the 1996 season got underway, and unlike the last three postseason years, the Braves got out of the gate quickly. A 16–11 April was followed by a 19–6 May, and as June began, the Braves had already opened up a five-game lead in the National League East. As title defenses go, this one was going great.

Even injuries didn't slow down the team. When David Justice was sidelined by a shoulder problem in mid-May, the Braves called up Jermaine Dye from Richmond. Dye made his debut on May 17 and promptly homered in his first major league at-bat, becoming the first Brave to do so since Chuck Tanner with the 1955 Milwaukee team.

Whenever a Braves player had a milestone moment, we would have our radio producer make a copy of the radio call and we would give it to the player. I know some players got major mileage from these keepsakes.

When Darrell Chaney was a member of our broadcast crew, he and his wife, Cindy, had a party during the off-season at their home. When Elaine and I arrived, we rang the doorbell. But instead of hearing the usual "ding-dong," we heard Marty Brennaman's radio call of Darrell's one and only major league grand slam home run. I hope some of our players were able to enjoy our call of their moment as much as Darrell did.

While Dye made numerous contributions to the Braves during the 1996 season, hitting .281 with 12 home runs, the rookie we were most anxiously awaiting didn't arrive until August. He was worth the wait.

We began hearing about Andruw Jones from the day he was signed as a 17-year-old from Curacao in 1994. Player personnel director Paul Snyder called Andruw "the best prospect the Braves have ever signed."

He would always have good things to say about our draft picks or free agents. But this was the most excited I'd ever seen him about a new player. It didn't take long for Paul's words to be proven right.

After hitting .290 in rookie league ball in 1994, Jones moved up to Class A Macon in '95. There he hit 25 home runs and drove in 100, earning himself *Baseball America's* Minor League Player of the Year award.

The following year, Andruw became just the second player to win that award twice (Gregg Jefferies in 1986 and '87 was the other), with a meteoric rise through the Braves' farm system. Jones began that year at Class A Durham, hitting .313 with 17 homers in just 66 games. Promoted to Double A Greenville, his numbers improved to .369 with 12 home runs in only 38 games. The next stop was Triple A Richmond, where the numbers continued to rise to .378, with five home runs in just 12 games.

In mid-August, at the age of 19, Andruw Jones was called up to Atlanta. He made his Braves debut on August 15 in an 8–5 win over the Phillies. He went 1-for-5 with a run-scoring single and a pair of strikeouts. The next evening, Jones hit his first major league home run in a 5–4 victory over Pittsburgh.

Atlanta already had a Gold Glove center fielder in Marquis Grissom, and Andruw spent his first major league season playing either left or right field. By season's end, he was hitting just .217. But with five home runs in 31 games—giving him 39 homers spread across four classifications for the season—and superb defensive play, he had given the team a glimpse of the star player he was to become.

The Braves, meanwhile, continued their dominance. They clinched their fifth consecutive division title with a week still remaining in the regular season. Another October was about to begin.

The Braves drew the Los Angeles Dodgers as their National League Division Series opponent and quickly dispatched them in a three-game sweep. Atlanta batted just .180 and scored only 10 runs in those three games, but that was more than enough for the Braves' vaunted starting rotation.

In Game 1 at Dodger Stadium, John Smoltz helped the Braves continue their one-run postseason one-upmanship. The dominant pitcher in baseball that season, Smoltz out-dueled Ramon Martinez, 2–1. He pitched nine innings of four-hit, one-run ball and got the victory after Javy Lopez homered in the top of the tenth and Mark Wohlers came on to get the save.

Despite another great outing by Greg Maddux, the Braves trailed 2–1 in Game 2 in Chávez Ravine until late-inning lightning struck twice in the seventh. Fred McGriff led off the inning with a home run and, one out later, Jermaine Dye took Ismael Valdez deep. When Wohlers preserved the 3–2 victory with another save, the Braves confidently flew home with a 2–0 advantage in the NLCS.

Game 3, in contrast, was a relative breeze. The Braves scored once in the first inning, then broke it open in the fourth on Mark Lemke's two-run double off Hideo Nomo and Chipper Jones' subsequent two-run home run. Tom Glavine allowed just one run in 6⅔ innings, and Wohlers' third save sent Atlanta on to its fifth consecutive NL Championship Series.

Dodgers first baseman Eric Karros summed up the series, "When you're facing a staff like Atlanta's, you're going to get two or three pitches to hit all day, and you've got to hit them. If you don't, you're in big trouble."

Next up for the Braves were the St. Louis Cardinals, who had swept the San Diego Padres in their Division Series. This series pitted managers Bobby Cox and Tony La Russa against each other in what was becoming a lifelong rivalry. While both men have tremendous respect for each other, they have never really liked one another.

Both men are excellent at what they do. Both are bound for the Hall of Fame. But their styles and personalities are total opposites. They are to managing what Milo Hamilton and Harry Caray were to broadcasting.

There's La Russa, the micro-manager with a law degree whose dugout always contains computer printouts of every conceivable matchup that may occur and whose calm demeanor rarely varies.

And there's Cox, more of the old-fashioned "seat-of-the-pants" type manager who relies on a feel for the game—and who possesses a very vocal demeanor whether it's encouraging his players or harassing an umpire.

In the NLCS opener in Atlanta-Fulton County Stadium, John Smoltz pitched very well again. But he needed a bases-loaded, two-run single in the eighth inning by Javy Lopez to beat the Cardinals 4–2. As usual, Wohlers recorded his fourth save in his fourth postseason opportunity, but Greg Maddux wasn't his usual self the following night.

St. Louis broke a 3–3 tie in the seventh inning of Game 2 to take a 4–3 lead. Then Gary Gaetti broke open the ballgame with a grand slam off Maddux, good for an 8–3 victory. As the series shifted to Busch Stadium, the momentum had shifted, too.

The Cardinals clearly appeared to have the Braves' number. In Game 3, former Brave Ron Gant hit two home runs off of Tom Glavine—a two-run homer in the first inning and a solo in the fifth—in that 3–2 St. Louis win. The next day, a future Brave, Brian Jordan, hit an eighth-inning home run off Greg McMichael, giving the Cardinals a 4–3 victory and a 3–1 lead in the series.

But faced with an unexpected early elimination and another loud, capacity crowd at Busch Stadium, the Braves stayed alive in Game 5. They jumped on right-hander Todd Stottlemyre, the Game 2 winner, for five runs in the first inning. They added two more runs in the second and another three in the fourth to make the score 10–0. The Braves were on their way to a 14–0 rout, and the NLCS was on its way back to Atlanta.

And once again, the momentum had shifted. The Braves pounded out a League Championship Series–record 22 hits—including four apiece by

Lemke and Lopez (who had two doubles and a home run) and a homer by McGriff.

Gaetti, the Cardinals' third baseman who crushed that grand slam in Game 2, summed up the Braves' show of power, "They not only set the table—they cleaned the dishes, too."

Back in Atlanta, the Braves turned to Maddux. He did not disappoint. Game 6 was vintage Mad Dog, as he shut out St. Louis through six innings and departed with two out in the eighth and a 2–1 lead. Maddux allowed just six hits and no walks and struck out seven Cardinals.

As for that lone St. Louis run in the eighth inning? It was scored on a wild pitch by Mark Wohlers—the only run the Cardinals would score in the last three games of the NLCS.

It was time for another Game 7, with the winner advancing to a World Series meeting with the New York Yankees. The Yankees, once World Series perennials, would be playing in their first Fall Classic since 1981. They had defeated the Baltimore Orioles in five games—including the infamous Jeffrey Maier incident in Game 1 of the ALCS.

This NLCS Game 7 was over almost immediately after it started. In the first inning, the Braves struck for six runs off of Cardinals starter Donovan Osborne. The last three scored on Tom Glavine's bases-loaded triple past a diving Gant. By the seventh-inning stretch, with home runs by Fred McGriff, Javy Lopez, and Andruw Jones leading the way, the Atlanta lead was 13–0.

Then came one of my favorite moments ever during my career with the Braves.

Normally, during the seventh-inning stretch, the crowd stands and is asked to "Join in the singing of 'Take Me Out to the Ballgame.'" But on this night, a different song was played. As the fans began to rise, the familiar opening bars of Frank Sinatra's "New York, New York" rang throughout Atlanta-Fulton County Stadium. The crowd needed no further prompting. By the time Ol' Blue Eyes invited everyone to "Start spreading the news," more than 52,000 voices were singing along. It was one of the greatest sights and sounds I've ever experienced.

By the end of the evening, the 15–0 drubbing of the Cardinals had the Braves headed for their fourth World Series in five seasons—this time against October's most hallowed franchise, the New York Yankees.

The Braves had become the first National League team to overcome a 3–1 deficit in the Championship Series and win the pennant. In so doing, they also became the first National League club to win four pennants in five completed seasons since the Brooklyn Dodgers in 1952-53-55-56.

Javy Lopez was voted the NLCS Most Valuable Player after hitting .542 (13-for-24) with five doubles, two home runs, and six RBIs.

Whether you are a player, a fan, or a broadcaster, there is nothing quite like a World Series game at Yankee Stadium—especially if you grew up in the fifties, as I did, when you might have thought that the Series was always played in the Bronx. The history, the tradition, the electricity of the crowd, Bob Sheppard's distinctive public address voice—even though we had become somewhat accustomed to playing in the Fall Classic, this felt like the first *real* one.

And what a start it was for Atlanta. On a clear, crisp October evening, picking up right where they'd left off against the Cardinals, the Braves continued their torrid hitting pace, pummeling the Yankees 12–1. Andruw Jones quickly set one World Series record and tied another when he homered in his first two World Series at-bats. The first, off Andy Pettitte, made him—at 19 years, six months, and 28 days—the youngest player ever to hit a World Series homer. Jones came in several months younger than 20-year-old Mickey Mantle in 1952.

Andruw's second home run added his name alongside Gene Tenace of the 1972 Oakland A's as the only players to homer in their first two World Series at-bats.

We worked the game on radio, and I did the call on Jones' second home run. I asked our listeners, "After his meteoric rise through our farm system, from Macon to Durham to Greenville to Richmond, does Andruw realize there's no higher league he can go to?"

After the game, Andruw was escorted into the media interview room, where he unwittingly broke up the horde of reporters with one of his answers. Asked who his baseball idol was as a youngster, Andruw gave it considerable thought. The assembled media waited patiently, wondering which baseball icon he would name: Mickey Mantle? Willie Mays? Who would it be?

When Andruw finally answered, "I don't know…Ken Griffey Jr.?" the room erupted in laughter. Griffey was only 26 years old. But Andruw was just 19 and during his high school years, Griffey had already emerged as a major league star. When you thought about it, the answer made sense. But it certainly wasn't what you were expecting to hear.

The opening of the Series in New York also afforded me the opportunity to close the door on one more question regarding my father. It was earlier that year when my mother had sent me the copy of Howard's death certificate. I had jotted down his last known address and stuck it in my wallet.

While riding to Yankee Stadium on the day of Game 1, I noticed that the team bus was proceeding up Madison Avenue. I pulled out the note I had made. I was looking for 1545. When you proceed north through Manhattan's Upper East Side, there comes a point right around 96th Street when you suddenly leave the trendy, fashionable part of town and enter a totally different world.

It was after passing this point that I found the address I was looking for. It was a nondescript six-story building, part of the Carver Homes public housing project. I stared at the building as we passed.

"So this is where he was," I thought to myself. "So this was his world."

As we passed by, I looked at the people on the street, many of whom appeared to be doing little more than hanging out. I couldn't help but think, "If I had been making this ride 25 years ago, would one of those people have been my father?" The thought gave me chills.

Throughout the rest of my career, as I'd done that day, whenever the Braves had a game at Yankee Stadium, I always made it a point to sit on the side of the bus where I could stare at this building—1545 Madison Avenue—as we passed. I normally sat on the right side of the bus. But on the return trip to the hotel, I would move and sit on the left so I could see 1545 Madison Avenue again. It's hard to describe the haunted, hollow feelings I had each and every time.

A second trip past this spot brought us back to Yankee Stadium for Game 2, where once again the Braves prevailed. Greg Maddux shut down the Yankee bats in a 4–0 win that was far more decisive than the final score suggested. In eight innings, he allowed just six hits and walked no one.

How masterfully did he pitch? Of the 24 outs Maddux recorded, he struck out just two Yankees. Twenty-one other outs came on ground balls. Five of those outs were little comeback grounders to the mound that Maddux—a perennial Gold Glove winner—seemed able to grab against any team he faced.

Fred McGriff drove in three of Atlanta's four runs in Game 2. Coupled with his two RBIs in the opener, that gave McGriff 15 RBIs during the '96 postseason, a new major league record. He'd add one more RBI—but only one—before the World Series was over.

During their last five games, the Braves had outscored the Cardinals and Yankees by an astounding 48–2. With the lineup so potent and pitching so dominant, we were now just two more victories away from another World Series title—and we were heading back to Atlanta.

But it was back home where the Series took an unexpected turn. David Cone out-dueled Tom Glavine in Game 3, giving the Yankees their first win, 5–2.

In Game 4, Denny Neagle was making his first start of the postseason. The Braves quickly staked him to an early lead with a four-run second inning (including a McGriff solo homer off Kenny Rogers and Marquis Grissom's two-run double), then added single runs in both the third and fifth to make it 6–0. Neagle was throwing a two-hit shutout.

Even after the Yankees cut the lead in half with a three-run sixth, Atlanta still carried a 6–3 lead into the eighth inning. It's an inning most Braves fans will never forget.

For one of the few times all season, Bobby Cox brought in closer Mark Wohlers to start the eighth. With two Yankees on and one out, Joe Torre sent up Jim Leyritz to pinch-hit. Leyritz, a good fastball hitter, fouled off a couple of Wohlers' 90+ mph heaters. After fouling off a slider to stay alive, Leyritz then jumped on a hanging slider. He drilled it over the left field wall for a three-run homer and a 6–6 tie. The crowd was stunned.

Wohlers escaped another jam in the ninth when the Yankees loaded the bases with two outs before Jermaine Dye caught Mariano Duncan's line drive to right. There was no escaping in the tenth, however. Not after Steve Avery came on in a rare relief appearance. Not after the Yankees scored twice on a bases-loaded walk and an error by Ryan Klesko to win 8–6 and even the Series at two games apiece.

For years after that game, Wohlers, who could hit 100 mph on the radar gun with his fastball, had to answer the question, "Why did you throw Leyritz a slider?" There was no fault to admit.

Wohlers' 90 mph slider was normally quite an effective pitch.

Leyritz simply caught one and gave it a ride.

With the Series now tied, Game 5 turned into one of the best-ever World Series pitching duels between two pitchers destined to become the winningest pitchers in postseason history. This time, Andy Pettitte bested John Smoltz, 1–0, giving the Yankees a 3–2 Series lead.

The only run of the night came in the fourth inning when Grissom, the Gold Glove center fielder, dropped a Charlie Hayes fly ball in right-center after nearly colliding with right fielder Jermaine Dye.

Hayes later scored on a double by Cecil Fielder. It appeared to many that Dye had crossed in front of Grissom, obscuring his vision just before the ball hit his glove and fell to the ground. But Grissom refused to blame the rookie, insisting that he should have caught the ball and that the error was his fault and his alone.

It was the final game ever played in Atlanta-Fulton County Stadium. In the first-ever major league game played there, Tony Cloninger was the starting pitcher for the Braves and Joe Torre was his catcher. In this one, 31 seasons later, Torre was the Yankees manager and Cloninger was his bullpen coach.

That unearned run in the fourth inning stood up. It not only gave the Yankees a 1–0 victory and a 3–2 lead in the Series, it also prevented Smoltz from having a shot at his 30th win of the season. He would be the runaway National League Cy Young Award winner that year, going 24–8. Smoltz would go on to win one game in the Division Series, two more in the NLCS and Game 1 of the World Series against the Yankees—and he was also the winning pitcher in that year's All-Star Game.

All combined, Smoltz went 29–9 that season and had pitched 293⅔ innings.

As we were boarding the flight back to New York for Game 6, we were all congratulating John on his remarkable year. That's when he made this totally understandable remark:

"I gave it all I had. There's not a drop left in the tank."

Back in the Bronx for Game 6, the Braves were unable to reverse the momentum. There was no stopping the Yankees now. This time, they got to Maddux early, scoring three runs in the third inning. The big hit was a triple by the Yankees' light-hitting catcher Joe Girardi, who had been one of Greg's catchers with the Chicago Cubs and is now the Yankees' manager.

Although the Braves scored once in the fourth inning and closed the gap to 3–2 in the ninth when Charlie Hayes caught a foul pop to end the game, the loss gave the Yankees their 23rd world championship. It was a bittersweet ending for all of us.

I was on the air for that final out, and I remember thinking, "*Am I a jinx?*" I had the final out in Minnesota in '91, I had the final out against Toronto in '92, and now I had the final out that sent us home in '96. If I had been on the air in '92 and '95, would Sid Bream have been out at the plate and would Marquis Grissom have dropped that ball?

I didn't seriously believe that, but the thought crossed my mind.

Disappointment was certainly present for us after coming so close to a second straight World Series title. Yet you couldn't help but feel good for Joe Torre, our friend and former manager who finally had his first world championship and something more valuable.

On the off day between Games 5 and 6, Joe's older brother, Frank, another former Brave and Joe's hero as a child, received a life-saving heart transplant in New York City. Some things are bigger than the outcome of a ballgame.

Chapter **12**

Other Sports, Other Venues

T he frustration of letting that 1996 World Series slip away lingered with players, coaches, and fans all winter long. But as a broadcaster, there was hardly time to think about it. Ever since I entered the business in 1965, as soon as one season ended, it was time to move on to the next sport.

While I was primarily employed as a baseball broadcaster, I also spent 30 years calling other sports when baseball was idle. Just a few days after the 1996 World Series ended, I was on a plane bound for Tokyo to handle TNT's coverage of a pair of regular-season NBA games between the New Jersey Nets and Orlando Magic at the Tokyo Dome.

I worked NBA games for 20 years beginning in 1976 when Ted Turner asked me if I had ever done any basketball. Atlanta Hawks games were being simulcast, and Ted wanted separate broadcasts for radio and TV. I told him that I had basketball experience dating back to 1966 when I did some high school games in Manassas, Virginia. After moving to Binghamton later that year, I began a five-year stint as play-by-play man for Broome Tech, one of the top junior college programs in the country. The Hornets were coached by Dick Baldwin, who, in a 45-year career—all but five at the junior college level— amassed 961 wins.

That's 59 more than Bobby Knight.

Dick turned down numerous offers to move to a four-year school—and when he finally did, it was only across town to Binghamton University, a Division III program at the time. I learned a lot from this legendary coach—most importantly to prepare the same for every game, no matter how big or small.

The Hawks had a limited TV schedule in the mid-1970s, usually about 30 games a season. Initially, I did the radio while Skip handled the TV call. That schedule gradually increased when TBS began expanding on cable. By the mid-1980s, the Hawks were moved to a regional television network as TBS began its partnership with the NBA, televising two to four games a week. I became a part of that coverage, and for the next ten years I worked about 25 games a season, including the playoffs.

This was a golden age for the NBA. Our games featured Michael Jordan, Larry Bird, Magic Johnson, Kareem Abdul-Jabbar, Charles Barkley, Isiah Thomas, Karl Malone, Patrick Ewing, Dominique Wilkins, and many more.

On occasion, one of these players would give you an insight into what made them great. During one season with the Hawks, we were playing the Boston Celtics in Hartford, Connecticut, on December 10, 1985. The radio station called and asked me to go to the Hartford Civic Center early. There was a problem with the phone lines and they wanted to make sure we'd be able to get on the air.

I walked over at about 4:00 PM to meet with a man from the telephone company to check it out. It was still three-and-a-half hours until tipoff. Besides the arena employees, there was no one there but us and a solitary figure who was slowly dribbling a basketball back and forth from one sideline to the other, gradually working his way down the court.

It was Larry Bird. When he came close to where we were standing, I asked him, "What are you doing?"

He chuckled and said, "Every time we play here, there's a couple of loose boards on this court. I want to make sure I know where they are." Attention to detail like that helped make Larry Bird Larry Bird.

Television was a different world. An NBA telecast was a day-long event. In the morning, you would go to each team's shoot-around—another term for morning practice—meet with each of the coaches, and then proceed back to the hotel for a production meeting. Usually over lunch, a game plan would be developed for the telecast. Then it was back to the room for a little more homework before finally heading to the game.

That was the routine we followed on April 29, 1992, when Hubie Brown and I were in Los Angeles to cover Game 3 in the opening round of the playoff series between the Lakers and the Portland Trailblazers.

The Blazers held a 2–0 lead in the best-of-five series; thus, the Lakers were playing for their playoff lives. About 45 minutes before airtime, we were at the broadcast table at the Forum going over our notes when our producer, Scott Cockerill, asked us to come to the TV truck. This was a very unusual request so close to game time, but Hubie and I did as asked and walked back to the truck.

When we got there, we were directed to a couple of TV monitors that were tuned to local newscasts.

"I just want you guys to be aware of what's going on just a few blocks away," Scott said.

What was going on was the start of one of the most destructive civic uprisings in U.S. history. That afternoon, a Los Angeles jury had acquitted four police officers, who had been accused of beating Rodney King during an arrest. The verdict was not what the residents of South Central LA wanted to hear.

Angry mobs were assembling in the streets and attacking vehicles and people. At that moment, it was confined to several square blocks not far from the Forum.

We returned to the floor to work the game, but during every commercial break we were informed that the situation was getting worse. Even our scoreboard updates from Ernie Johnson Jr. back in our Atlanta studios included video from CNN of the fires that were erupting all over the area.

The game went on before a sellout crowd and went into overtime. With about a minute remaining in the OT, the Lakers had taken a 2-point lead and, with the crowd reaching its highest decibel level of the night, Portland called a time out.

At that moment, the public address announcer silenced the jubilant gathering.

"Your attention please: please listen to the following instructions for exiting the parking lots after tonight's game…"

He then gave what was, in effect, a Forum evacuation plan—to get this crowd safely out of harm's way. All traffic would be funneled onto Manchester Avenue and that would be the only route available to get you to one of the LA freeways.

The game resumed—the Lakers held on to win, 121–119—and after wrapping up the broadcast, Hubie and I headed back to the truck. The TV monitors were again tuned in to local newscasts, and we were appalled at how the situation had deteriorated.

Exiting the parking lot took nearly an hour because all cars were being directed onto the same road. Once you reached Manchester Avenue, police in full riot gear were lining the street to protect exiting traffic from the angry hordes that were roaming, looting, and burning large sections of South Central LA.

At one point, a group of these angry demonstrators tipped over a large trash bin and rolled it into the street causing us to swerve to avoid being hit. We finally reached the freeway and drove back to our hotel in Marina Del Rey shaken by the experience.

Not everybody in our group got away unscathed. A van driven by Cockerill and his assistant, Marc Silverman, had something shatter the rear windshield. "I didn't know if we had gotten shot or what," Scott said. "I just went pedal to the metal and got us the hell out of there."

Back at the hotel, we went to the rooftop bar, which offered a view of the city. You could see fires burning all over that portion of town.

Smoke was everywhere the next morning. The airport is not far from the scene of the worst rioting, and it was quite harrowing just returning the rental car. While driving down the access road to the rental lot, we passed a convenience store where we noticed someone walking on the roof with what looked like a rifle. We hoped that it was either a police officer or the store owner protecting his property.

When we reached the terminal at LAX, all flights were delayed. We finally got out of there by mid-afternoon, about four hours late. When we took off, we looked down on a smoke-filled city that was still four days away from quieting down.

That was not the only unusual travel experience I had. The only team flight I ever missed was an Atlanta Hawks flight from Cleveland to Atlanta on February 21, 1972. At that time, the NBA had a rule that if you were playing in back-to-back nights in different cities, you had to fly on the first available commercial flight to the second city. Teams weren't chartering yet.

Our flight was scheduled to leave Cleveland at 7:00 AM that Saturday morning after our game with the Cavaliers the night before. I slept right through the alarm and woke up at 7:20. I remember exactly what time it was, realizing I had missed the flight. The first thing I did was to call Delta to see if by chance the flight might be leaving late. No, I was told, it took off on time. I then began to arrange to get on the next available flight back to Atlanta.

"You already have a ticket for the 12:00 flight," I was told. Joe O'Toole, the Hawks trainer and travel manager, had left my ticket at the airport when I didn't show up. Knowing that I was in for major harassment from all involved, I spent a leisurely morning having breakfast at the hotel, reading the paper, and calling the Hawks' office to let them know I was okay. I went to Hopkins Airport, boarded my flight, and took off right on time.

When I landed in Atlanta at about 2:00, the first thing I did was call the Hawks to let them know I was here. The secretary said, "You're *here*? How could you be here? The team's not!"

I said, "What do you mean the team's not?"

The Hawks' 7:00 AM flight had been diverted to Birmingham due to bad weather in Atlanta. As it turned out, my flight was one of the first to be allowed to land once Hartsfield Airport reopened. Since the team wasn't sure if or when they'd be able to get out of Birmingham, they had ordered a bus to come and pick them up.

When I got to the Omni at about 5:00, they still weren't there.

Finally, at about 5:30, as bedraggled-looking a bunch of travelers as you've ever seen arrived at the arena. When they saw me all set up and ready to go courtside, they were astonished—and a bit miffed.

Hubie Brown, who was the Hawks head coach at the time, came right over and said, "Where were you? How did you get here?" I said, "I was about to ask you the same question." Hubie didn't think it was funny.

For weeks after that, I was reminded of the lovely day of travel that I'd missed with the rest of the guys. I also decided that if I ever had to miss a flight—that was the one to miss.

My NBA years also included a couple of international assignments. In October 1990, I went to Barcelona to cover the McDonald's Open, an annual event that featured one team from the NBA and three European professional teams. That year, it was the New York Knicks and teams from Spain, Italy, and Yugoslavia.

The tournament was the inaugural event at the Palau Saint Jordi, one of the principle venues for the 1992 Summer Olympics. The team representing Spain was the Regal FC Barcelona team from the Spanish League. We learned that they would be playing a regular league game the night before the tournament started. Doug Collins, Mike Fratello, and I decided to go to that game to familiarize ourselves with the Spanish team.

This game was played at the Palau Blaugrana, a much smaller and older arena. What an entertaining evening that turned out to be. The crowd of about 5,000 was much more animated than what we were used to seeing. Whenever Barcelona got a scoring run going, they would begin that chant often heard at soccer games:

"O-laaaay—ole, ole, O-laaaay......O-laaaay......O-laaaay!"

They were having so much fun, even we joined in.

Toward the end of the game, a referee's call went against Barcelona, and fans began throwing items onto the court—paper, cans, just trash. Suddenly, a floor-to-ceiling net was raised, completely surrounding the court. The game finished with the teams playing safely inside this cage.

The crowds were much more subdued for the actual tournament, which the Knicks won. They beat a Yugoslavian team that featured a young Toni Kucoc, still a year away from becoming an NBA player. He was a tall, outside shooting forward who became a key part of the Chicago Bulls NBA championship run.

In 1996, I was assigned to cover a couple of regular season games between the New Jersey Nets and the Orlando Magic in Tokyo. We were amazed at the interest in the NBA by Japanese fans and how familiar they seemed to be with so many of the players. The games were played at the Tokyo Dome, home of the Tokyo Giants baseball team, and the crowds were huge. Nearly 40,000 attended each game. NBA merchandise sold out almost as quickly as it arrived.

As much fun as it was doing events like these, my greatest enjoyment during my NBA years was working in such classic places as the old Boston Garden, Madison Square Garden, and Chicago Stadium. These were the vintage arenas, where so much NBA history had been made, and just having the opportunity to work a game in them was a great thrill.

It was also a privilege to work with so many outstanding broadcast partners. During the regular season, I was paired at times with Rick Barry, Steve Jones, Doug Collins, Hubie Brown, Jack "Goose" Givens, Mike Glenn, and Dick Versace. All of them were terrific, especially Hubie Brown. He is one of the best prepared and most well-versed analysts I've ever worked with in any sport.

Any year when the playoffs began, TBS and TNT would do as many as four games a night between them. They'd add active coaches whose teams were out of the playoff picture to the broadcast roster. This gave me a chance to work a game each with Don Nelson, John MacLeod, Mike Fratello, Doc Rivers, and Chuck Daly.

I was always a little nervous about these games. These men were so much closer to the game than I was. I didn't want to ask them the wrong question or lead them in the wrong direction. But apparently, they felt the same way about working on a national broadcast.

To a man, they each asked me when the game was over, "How'd I do? Did I do all right?"

Football was another sport where I spent many years as a broadcaster. It started with high school games in Warrenton, Virginia. In Binghamton, New York, I would broadcast as many as three high school games on a single weekend—one on Friday night, one on Saturday afternoon, and a third on Saturday night.

When Ted Turner secured the television rights for the Atlanta Falcons' preseason games in 1977, I was assigned to them. At that time, the National Football League had a six-game preseason schedule, not four.

Ex-Falcon running back Harmon Wages was the analyst in 1977, and in 1978, Tommy Nobis, the great Falcons linebacker and the team's original No. 1 draft pick in its first season, assumed that role. One of the 1978 games was played against the Pittsburgh Steelers at Three Rivers Stadium. During one Falcons possession, quarterback Steve Bartkowski was sacked, hit simultaneously by "Mean Joe" Greene and Jack Lambert.

In the slow-motion replay, there is a moment when Greene and Lambert, in lockstep, are just about to get to Bartkowski. Tommy's description was wonderful:

"Right about here, ol' Steve really feels like he is going to...go to the bathroom."

I'm glad Tommy phrased it that way, but I still had a difficult time controlling my laughter.

The expansion on cable of TBS forced the Falcons to move their preseason games to one of the local Atlanta channels in 1979. NFL owners did not want out-of-market exhibition games televised in their city.

The next football game that I broadcast was the 1979 Independence Bowl in Shreveport, Louisiana. It was a matchup between Syracuse and McNeese State, and former Washington Redskins quarterback Billy Kilmer was my analyst.

Frank Maloney was the head coach at Syracuse and guided his team to a 31–7 victory. The great wide receiver Art Monk caught a couple of touchdown passes. Two years later, Maloney was fired. The next time I saw Frank was 1982 in the press lounge at Wrigley Field. That was so odd. I walked in there and saw him and thought he was there to throw out the first ball or something. As I talked to him, I thought to myself, "He's working here now."

After being fired by Syracuse, Maloney decided to leave football altogether. So he returned to his hometown and joined the Chicago Cubs group sales department. Frank is now the Director of Ticket Sales for the Cubs. It still strikes me as an unusual career move.

In 1985, TBS signed a two-year deal with the Big Ten Conference for a Game of the Week that was syndicated to about 100 stations nationwide. My broadcast partner for these games was Ron Kramer, the one-time University of Michigan All-American and former Detroit Lions tight end.

We had a ball for those two years. There is nothing quite like a football weekend on a Big Ten college campus. Whether it's the 100,000-plus crowds at Michigan Stadium in Ann Arbor, the Purdue band marching toward and then into Ross-Ade Stadium with the "World's Largest Drum," or the tuba in the Ohio State band dotting the "i" in the script Ohio in the Big Horseshoe, there was great tradition and excitement every week, everywhere.

In addition, Ron seemingly knew everyone in the Midwest, and the perks were outstanding. One of those perks was our weekly golf outing. We would arrive in the game city on Thursday night. Friday morning, Ron and I would meet with the home team's head coach. Friday evening we would get together with the visiting head coach at his team's hotel. Saturday was game day, and then we would fly home.

In between the coaches meetings on Friday, we played a round of golf.

Kramer had contacts everywhere and got us onto some outstanding courses. One weekend in Minneapolis was particularly memorable. We met that Friday morning with University of Minnesota head coach Lou Holtz, an extremely entertaining man. The Gophers were playing Michigan the next day for the Little Brown Jug, another outstanding Big Ten tradition. After meeting with Lou, we were off to the Golden Valley Country Club. There we met our host, Max McGee, the former Green Bay Packers star and a good friend of Ron's. Max introduced us to the other member of our foursome, Gene Okerlund. Known to professional wrestling fans as "Mean Gene," he was perhaps the best-known wrestling announcer in the world.

The teams were chosen: Ron and I against Max and Mean Gene. As we were loosening up on the first tee, Max proposed the terms of the match.

"Best-ball. Half a buck a hole okay with everybody?"

Everyone nodded yes, and off we went.

By the time we reached the 18th hole, Ron and I were each down 50 cents. We had halved the last three holes, so there were four holes riding on number 18, a par 5.

Max, Gene, and I each reached the final green in regulation. Ron was lying 3 in a greenside bunker. His fourth shot stopped about 15 feet beyond the hole.

The rest of us were each about 25-30 feet away. Both Max and Gene just barely missed their birdie putts and had easy tap-ins for par. My birdie attempt rolled about 4 feet past the pin.

When Ron lipped out his par putt, it was all up to me.

"Have you ever had to make a putt for this much money, Petey?" Ron asked. He always called me Petey.

I laughed. "What…$2?" I asked.

Ron came up alongside me and in a deadly serious tone said, "Petey…if you miss this putt, it'll cost us each 200 bucks."

I had suddenly learned a stunning, potentially painful lesson. In gambler's parlance, "half a buck" means $50.

We were not down 50 cents. We were down $50. This was not a $2 putt; this was a $200 4-footer. To make matters worse, I was only carrying about $120 in cash. What the hell was I going to do if I missed it?

I could literally feel my legs shaking as I stood over that 4-foot putt, which now looked more like a 40-footer. I don't recall anything else about the next few seconds. But I do remember the beautiful sight of that golf ball dropping into the cup for my par.

To this day, I consider that the greatest achievement of my athletic career.

I loved everything about those college football weekends. And I was sorry when the Big Ten formed its own network in 1987, ending our association.

There was, however, one more stop in my football broadcasting career.

In 1987, Sportschannel Florida was launched. One of its producers was Harlan Senger, a former Turner employee. He got permission from TBS to use Turner personnel on a limited freelance basis until the new cable channel developed a full staff. Harlan hired me to do University of Florida football and basketball games.

The football games were tape-delayed for replay on Sportschannel that night—or, in the event of a night game, the following day. The basketball broadcasts were limited to non-conference games but were aired live.

Working with Jim Yarbrough (another former Detroit Lion) on the football broadcasts and Bill Koss on basketball games, I spent two years commuting back and forth between Atlanta and Gainesville during the baseball off-season. My two sons, Jon and Steve, both University of Georgia students at the time, couldn't believe their father was a broadcaster for their arch-rival. The irony was that the dollars earned by broadcasting those Gators games helped pay their Georgia tuitions.

The most memorable event during the two years I spent with the Gators occurred Thanksgiving week of 1988, when I accompanied the basketball team to Anchorage, Alaska. They were there to play in the Great Alaskan Shootout. The eight-team field included Kansas, Kentucky, and Seton Hall, the tournament's eventual winner.

Tournaments such as these are a great opportunity to get together with broadcasters and writers from all over the country, to talk about the games, the teams, the players, and the business.

What was astonishing to all of us was the popularity of the Braves…in Anchorage, Alaska! Everywhere we went, I was recognized, and people wanted to talk about the Braves. TBS used to replay the Braves telecasts at 1:00 AM EST. This was prime time—9:00 PM—in Anchorage, and ratings there and throughout the state of Alaska were huge. It was an impressive reminder of what Ted Turner's cable TV experiment had become.

In 1984, TBS was selected to televise the championship game of the Amateur Baseball World Series in Havana, Cuba. That experience was among the most memorable of my career. The powerful 1984 U.S. Olympic team, which featured such future major league stars as Mark McGwire, Will Clark, and Barry Larkin, had been disassembled at the end of the '84 Summer Games.

A new team was put together for this October event. Among those making the Havana trip was a young outfielder from Arizona State named Barry Bonds.

The TBS traveling party consisted of me, a technical director, a unit manager, and an interpreter. The bulk of our crew would be locals employed by Cuban National Television.

A couple of Cuban state officials were with us at all times and seemed very suspicious of all of us. When we wanted to check out our broadcast setup at Latin American Stadium, they would ask, "Why? There is no game being played there now."

When we asked to visit with Team USA personnel to get more information on the team, we were told, "They may not be in the championship game. There is no need for that now."

I don't know if they thought we were terrorists in disguise or what. But we were only allowed to go where they wanted us to go and when they wanted to take us.

We were finally taken to the ballpark the day before the championship game. At last, we were able to make contact with Team USA. We were shown the broadcast booth to which we were assigned, but when we got there the next day for the broadcast, they had moved us elsewhere.

Team USA did make it to the finals, where they would play Cuba. We learned Fidel Castro would be attending the game. I asked if there was any possibility we could get an interview with him. The state official answered with an icy stare, "You know, of course, there have been plots by your country to assassinate our president. Such a request is not possible."

I guess that meant "No."

Cuba defeated the United States for the championship. After the game, Castro went onto the field to present the gold medals to the Cuban players and silver medals to the Americans. We taped the ceremony for airing the next day, but when we got back to Atlanta and looked at the tape, the Cuban TV crew had deleted the Team USA presentation. I have no idea why.

Outside of the paranoia displayed by the government officials who were constantly with us, we found Cuba to be a land of warm and friendly people. We were appalled by some of the poverty we saw, troubled by the lack of such common items as paper and glass, but impressed by the ingenuity of the people.

Automobiles from the 1950s were still running. Newspapers, while scarce, were never thrown away. They were either passed along to someone else or saved for, uh, other purposes. And somehow, baseball fans were pretty well informed on major league players and teams despite having virtually no legal means of gaining such information.

All of these off-season assignments ended in 1997. While I enjoyed all of them and the variety, the year-round travel was beginning to wear on me. It was time to cut back. Turner Sports was evolving, as well.

There were more and more employees assigned year-round to a specific sport. There were fewer and fewer, especially on the announcer side, doing "double duty."

When spring training began in 1997, I was back to my first love—broadcasting baseball exclusively.

Chapter **13**

The Bridesmaid Years

By 1997, the Braves were well established as the "Team of the Nineties." The slogan is even inscribed on the side of the 1995 World Championship ring. That high level of excellence continued for the rest of the decade and on into the next. But as the streak of division championships mounted, so did the frustration with the Braves' inability to win another World Series title.

In 1997, we had new spring training digs, moving from West Palm Beach to Disney World. We also moved into our new home in Atlanta—Turner Field, which had been reconfigured after serving as the Olympic Stadium for the 1996 centennial Summer Games. Opening night included a ceremony where Tom Glavine walked through an opening in the outfield wall and through a *Field of Dreams* cloud, carrying home plate from the old ballpark to the new one.

By the 11th game of the season, the Braves had moved into first place in the NL East Division and never looked back.

A mid-season trade with the Pittsburgh Pirates a year earlier had added left-hander Denny Neagle to the already strong starting rotation—arguably baseball's best. In his first full season in Atlanta, Neagle was the National League's only 20-game winner, going 20–5 with a 2.97 ERA.

The Braves' balanced offense featured seven different players who each reached double figures in home runs. Even Rafael Belliard hit his first homer in nearly a decade—and just the second, and last, of his career—one Friday night in a late-season game at Shea Stadium. Afterward in the clubhouse, teammates held up bats and crossed them for Raffy to walk beneath. Then they wrapped him in white tape and, for good measure, taped him inside his locker.

Spirits were high for Atlanta. Another trip to the World Series certainly seemed feasible.

The Braves wasted little time disposing of Houston, the NL Central champions, in the Division Series. They outscored the Astros, 19–5, and never trailed in a three-game sweep—the second straight year Atlanta had swept an NLDS series. The Maddux-Glavine-Smoltz trio completely silenced the bats of the Astros' "Killer Bees." Jeff Bagwell, Craig Biggio, and Derek Bell were a combined 2–37 without a single extra-base hit or an RBI.

Maddux threw a complete-game seven-hitter in the opener and won, 2–1, on Ryan Klesko's solo homer in the second inning. Game 2 was no contest; the Braves broke a 3–3 tie with three runs in the fifth inning and five more in the sixth en route to a 13–5 rout. The Braves managed ten hits that day—the same number of walks they drew, including eight off of Houston starter Mike Hampton.

When John Smoltz threw a complete game in Game 3 and won, 3–1, the Braves were bound for a record sixth straight NLCS. The big three of Maddux, Glavine, and Smoltz had allowed just three earned runs in 24 innings against Houston and combined for a collective 1.87 ERA. That's how an offense that bats just .217 but scores 19 runs on 20 hits advances.

That set up an NLCS matchup with the Florida Marlins, who had likewise swept the San Francisco Giants. Although the Marlins had been in existence only five seasons, owner Wayne Huizenga had spent liberally to bring a contender to Miami, even signing Jim Leyland to manage.

After reaching the postseason as the National League's wild card team, the Marlins made the most of their playoff debut.

In the NLCS opener, Maddux faced Kevin Brown. Maddux had allowed just one unearned run all season. But the Marlins, with the help of two Braves errors, scored five unearned runs in the first inning and made them hold up in a 5–3 victory. Tom Glavine evened the series at a game apiece, easily winning

Game 2, 7–1, on homers by Ryan Klesko and Chipper Jones and with relief help from Mike Cather and Mark Wohlers.

Upon arrival in Florida, the Braves learned that the Marlins' number two starter, Alex Fernandez (17–12, 3.59), was out for the rest of the season. Fernandez had started Game 2 in Atlanta and was rocked for five runs in just 2⅔ innings. The next day, doctors determined that Fernandez had a torn rotator cuff. This was a severe blow to the Marlins. We felt better than ever about our chances.

Although Florida won Game 3, beating John Smotlz 5–2 on Charles Johnson's three-run double in the sixth inning, the Braves came right back the next day with a 4–0 victory on Neagle's four-hitter. When Brown, the Marlins' scheduled Game 5 starter, couldn't go due to illness, Leyland handed the ball to a 22-year-old rookie right-hander named Livan Hernandez.

The Braves starter was the four-time Cy Young Award–winner, future 300-game winner, and surefire Hall of Famer, Greg Maddux.

The home plate umpire was Eric Gregg, who became the key figure in the game. Gregg was a big man, who weighed well over 300 pounds. He was known for having a liberal strike zone. And on this day, that zone was almost as wide as he was.

This was especially true for left-handed hitters—of which the Braves had six—who repeatedly looked at pitches that appeared to be 8-12 inches outside, but were called strikes.

Don Sutton and I worked the first 4½ innings on radio. After turning it over to Skip and Joe, we went back to the press lounge to watch the rest of the game. One of the benefits of working alongside a Hall of Famer like Don was the insight he had in a game like this.

Recognizing the size of the strike zone early in the game, Don predicted, with near perfect accuracy, what the next pitch would be from both Hernandez and Maddux. For example, with two outs in the top of the ninth inning and the Marlins leading, 2–1, Hernandez got two strikes on Fred McGriff.

"All he has to do now," Don said, "is throw that curveball—it can be a foot outside, but as long as he doesn't bounce it, it'll be a strike."

Hernandez did just that—called strike three on McGriff—to record his 15th strikeout, an NLCS record. The 2–1 Florida victory left the Braves fuming and the Marlins up 3–2 in the series.

Many fans felt that Gregg's work behind the plate cost the Braves the game. But the strike zone was the same for both pitchers. The combined total for both teams that game was 25 strikeouts and only 3 walks.

Back in Atlanta for Game 6, the Marlins jumped on Tom Glavine for four first-inning runs. They added three more in the sixth and, behind Kevin Brown, who was back from the flu, won the game, 7–4, and took the series 4–2. The Marlins went on to beat the Cleveland Indians in a thrilling seven-game World Series and won the world championship.

It was the end of our first season at Turner Field, the first of many when we would watch another team celebrate on our turf.

The 1998 regular season was a cakewalk for the Braves, who set a franchise record with 106 wins and clinched their seventh consecutive division title with two weeks still remaining in the season.

The starting rotation was better than ever:

Tom Glavine was a 20-game winner for the fourth time in his career and captured his second Cy Young Award.

Greg Maddux went 18–9 with a league-leading 2.22 ERA.

John Smoltz was 17–3 with a 2.90 ERA

Denny Neagle followed up his 20-win season with a 16–11 mark.

And Kevin Millwood, the 23-year-old in his first full major league season, went 17–8.

It was only the second time in major league history that a team had five pitchers with 16 or more victories each. The first was the 1902 Pittsburgh Pirates. Remarkable!

This time, the NL Division Series opponent would be the Chicago Cubs, whose regular season was highlighted by Sammy Sosa and his home-run duel with Mark McGwire. Sosa finished with 66 homers, four behind McGwire. But only three had been hit off of Braves pitching.

Once again, the Division Series was over quickly. The Braves used their proven combination of Smoltz, Glavine, and Maddux to sweep the Cubs by scores of 7–1, 2–1, and 6–2. In the opener, Smoltz got an early two-run homer from Michael Tucker, then a seventh-inning insurance grand slam from Ryan Klesko.

The only real drama came in Game 2, a pitchers' duel between Glavine and the Cubs' Kevin Tapani. Javy Lopez hit a ninth-inning home run to send the game into extra innings. In the bottom of the tenth, Chipper Jones delivered a game-winning single to put the Braves up 2–0.

In Game 3 at Wrigley Field, Maddux scored the game's only run through seven innings after doubling off Cubs starter Kerry Wood in the third inning and later scoring on the rookie's wild pitch. In the eighth, Maddux got some breathing room from his personal catcher, Eddie Perez, who hit a grand slam to give Atlanta a 6–2 win. It was the Braves' tenth straight win in Division Series play.

The San Diego Padres came to Atlanta to open the NLCS on October 7 and left two days later with a 2–0 lead. Ken Caminiti's tenth-inning home run off Kerry Ligtenberg decided Game 1. Kevin Brown, now in a Padres uniform, shut out the Braves 3–0 in Game 2, striking out 11 with that devastating sinker.

The series moved to San Diego, where the Braves dropped a third straight game, 4–1. Atlanta left the bases loaded in the fourth, sixth, and eighth innings, stranding 12 runners overall.

In Game 4, it looked like the Braves were about to be swept out of town. They entered the seventh inning trailing 3–2. But in the top of the seventh, Andrés Galarraga, who was just 1-for-12 in the series to that point, hit a grand slam off Dan Miceli. The Braves held on for an 8–3 win, staying alive for Game 5.

The next night, the Braves struck late again. Trailing 4–2 in the eighth inning, Michael Tucker hit a three-run homer off Brown to give the Braves a 5–4 lead. When San Diego started a ninth-inning rally, Bobby Cox brought in Greg Maddux from the bullpen to preserve the win.

It was Greg's first relief appearance since 1987 and the only save of his career.

But the comeback magic, and the season, ended for the Braves when the series returned to Atlanta. In Game 6, the Braves managed just two hits off Sterling Hitchcock and a quartet of Padres relievers. San Diego broke a scoreless tie with five runs in the sixth and won 5–0.

And once again, we had to watch a Turner Field celebration by the visiting team.

* * *

In 1999, the Braves returned to the World Series—only to experience yet another frustrating and disappointing ending.

The year began on an ominous note in spring training when slugging first baseman Andres Galarraga was diagnosed with lymphoma, shelving him for the entire season. But the Braves plugged in Ryan Klesko and Randall Simon at the first base position. With its usual dominant starting pitching, the club posted its third straight 100-victory season, easily winning an eighth straight division title by seven games over the second-place New York Mets.

The NL Division Series featured a familiar opponent: Houston. The Astros managed one victory this time, but only one. Atlanta's 3–1 series victory was highlighted by Kevin Millwood's complete-game one-hitter in Game 2; Millwood's twelfth-inning save two days later, made possible by a spectacular tenth-inning defensive play by shortstop Walt Weiss; and the hitting heroics of Bret Boone, Brian Jordan, and Gerald Williams during the series.

That sent the Braves right back up against their division rivals, the Mets. New York, as the wild card team, had knocked out the NL West champion Arizona Diamondbacks in four games.

Atlanta quickly took a 3–0 lead in the NLCS as Maddux, Glavine, and Millwood limited the Mets to just five runs total in those three games. The Mets avoided being swept with a 3–2 victory in Game 4 at Shea Stadium. That was the lead-in to two of the most dramatic postseason games the Braves would ever play.

Game 5 began late in the afternoon of a cold and dreary day in Flushing, New York. It didn't end until nearly six hours later. In the top half of the fifteenth inning, Keith Lockhart tripled home Walt Weiss, who had walked, giving the Braves a 3–2 lead.

But in the bottom of the fifteenth, rookie reliever Kevin McGlinchy issued a bases-loaded walk to Todd Pratt, tying the game. The next hitter was Robin Ventura, who was just 1-for-18 at that point in the series. Ventura connected for a grand-slam home run over the right-center field wall. But he never made it beyond first base. As soon as the winning run crossed the plate, Ventura was literally tackled by his jubilant teammates.

The official final score was 4–3. It was the only time in my career that I ever saw a grand-slam single.

With the lead now three games to two, the Braves returned home for Game 6. Twice Atlanta had comfortable leads in that game, 5–0 after the first inning, 7–3 after six innings. But the Mets kept storming back. Once again, the game went into extra innings with the score tied, 8–8.

And once again, this time in the tenth inning, Todd Pratt delivered with a sacrifice fly that gave the Mets a 9–8 lead. But Ozzie Guillén's pinch-hit single off of Armando Benitez in the bottom of the tenth tied it up again.

Atlanta finally won the game, the series, and the pennant in the bottom half of the eleventh on one of the most unlikely walks ever. The free-swinging Andruw Jones drew a bases-loaded walk off Kenny Rogers.

Eddie Perez was named the NLCS Most Valuable Player.

The Braves were back in the World Series for the fifth time in nine years once again to take on New York's other team, the Yankees.

There was very little drama to the 1999 World Series. Those last two games with the Mets had drained the Braves' energy and emotion. The four-game sweep by the Yankees included only one close victory. That came in Game 3, when unheralded Chad Curtis hit a tenth-inning home run. His second homer of the game gave New York a 6–5 win.

I remember Braves general manager John Schuerholz boarding the team bus before Game 4. Skip asked him, "Well, John, what do you think?"

In a resigned tone, John answered, "It would be nice if we could win one game."

We couldn't.

The Nineties were over. And so, it turned out, were our World Series days.

*   *   *

While the 2000 season resulted in another division title and still another trip to postseason play, the most distinctive memories from that year involved neither.

The first actually dated back to the 1999 postseason, when Atlanta relief pitcher John Rocker became a favorite target of New York Mets and Yankees fans. Rocker's full-speed sprint from the bullpen to the mound, while popular at home, generated a totally opposite outburst from New York fans. Besides the usual boos, they threw things onto the field, cursed at him, and just let John know just how much they hated him.

In response, John antagonized them even further. When walking off the mound and back to the Braves dugout, he would spit at the fans, give them the finger, and do anything he could to exacerbate the situation.

Then the article came.

In December 1999, *Sports Illustrated* published a story by Jeff Pearlman in which Rocker unleashed a torrent of outrageous remarks about New York City. In those few pages, he vilified racial and ethnic groups, the gay community, single mothers, New York baseball fans, the No. 7 subway train that Mets fans ride to and from Shea Stadium, and virtually everything else about the city.

This rant so alarmed and angered Baseball Commissioner Bud Selig that he suspended Rocker for the first 30 days of the 2000 season for remarks "that offended practically every element of society." Selig also fined Rocker $20,000 and ordered him to undergo sensitivity training.

Hank Aaron brokered a meeting between Rocker and Andrew Young, the former United States ambassador to the United Nations and ex-mayor of Atlanta, whose long history in civil rights might serve as a beacon of change for John.

Rocker's teammates were noticeably quiet during this time. But that was understandable. John had broken the unwritten baseball code by ripping a teammate, Randall Simon, in the article. He also belittled the Braves' clubhouse atmosphere, comparing it to a "doctor's office."

The Player's Association, however, did come to Rocker's defense, appealing the punishment. An independent arbitrator reduced the suspension to 15 days and the fine to $500.

When Rocker reported to spring training in February 2000, he seemed to have little remorse for what had happened. In fact, he seemed to revel in the added attention he was getting.

All of this was infecting and distracting the team.

Rocker's suspension ended in mid-April, and he rejoined the Braves in Atlanta. There was no denying the left-hander's talent. Immediately returning to his role as closer, he reeled off three saves during the ten-game homestand. But on the first day of his first road trip of the season, more issues arose.

With the hungry media surrounding him, John repeated some of his boorish behavior, this time toward heckling fans at San Diego's Jack Murphy Stadium. When a *San Diego Union-Tribune* news photographer snapped a picture of this, Rocker railed at the man, ridiculing the individual's profession and income.

All of this was duly reported in the next day's *Union-Tribune*. When I read it, I was furious.

The Braves had tried to get Rocker on the high road to get him through this, but he kept adding to the problem. It was a ticklish situation for the team. They needed his talented left arm and his ability to close out games—but at what cost?

Normally, my three-minute "Diamond Notes" segment of the radio pregame show dealt with baseball history, trivia, or statistical perspectives on the game. As I sat down in my hotel room to prepare the April 29 show, I couldn't get this whole Rocker issue off my mind.

I wound up writing what was, in effect, an editorial chastising both Rocker for his lack of contrition and the Braves for allowing this situation to fester. I called John to task for thumbing his nose at any help the Braves tried to give him to get him through all this. I even questioned whether a Braves trip to another World Series wouldn't be somehow tainted if this Rocker situation went on all year.

My comments received national attention. This kind of subjectivity was out of character for my broadcast style. Most who heard it guessed—correctly—that there must be a real problem here.

I fully expected to be reprimanded by someone from the team for stating my personal opinion of the Rocker issue so strongly. But I heard I nothing—not from Bobby Cox, not from John Schuerholz, not from a single player. Nothing. It wasn't because they were unaware of what I had said. Even when they're not listening, baseball people have an uncanny ability to get reports on every word a broadcaster utters.

I had to believe that what I said pretty much reflected the unspoken thoughts of members of the Braves organization who had to deal with the Rocker dilemma every day. Later that season, Tom Glavine confirmed this when he told the *Atlanta Journal-Constitution*, "That, coming from Pete, meant something. It was like, hey, E.F. Hutton's talking. Let's listen."

One thing my criticism didn't do was change John's behavior. A couple of weeks later, Jeff Pearlman, who wrote the *Sports Illustrated* story, was in Atlanta on another assignment. When Rocker spotted him at Turner Field, he went ballistic, screaming and cursing at Pearlman, even threatening him. That outburst caused the Braves to send Rocker to the minor leagues for awhile, but he was back after a short stay and wound up leading Atlanta with 24 saves in 2000.

The situation grew gradually worse. The Braves had to order extra security for John whenever the team traveled to New York, which included an unmarked van to transport him to and from the stadium. In addition, a New York police officer would occupy the hotel room next to Rocker's during the duration of each stay. John also continued to blame teammates for games that got away from him. On one occasion, shortstop Ozzie Guillen just missed a ground ball up the middle that resulted in a game-winning hit for the Houston Astros. John's comment after the game was, "We had the wrong guy in there. Walt Weiss would've gotten to that ball."

These kinds of remarks continued to infuriate the other players. The Braves' patience finally ran out in June of the following year. Even though Rocker had a team-leading 19 saves at the time, he was traded to Cleveland.

The second story that developed during the 2000 season involved a part of the playing field that hardly ever gets mentioned—the catcher's box. On the weekend of June 23-25, the Milwaukee Brewers were the visiting team at Turner Field. After the Friday night game had ended, we noticed Brewers manager Davey Lopes meeting at home plate with the umpire crew chief, John Shulock. They were looking and gesturing at the area just behind home plate where the catcher squats.

Baseball rules dictate that this chalked-in box behind home plate be exactly 43 inches wide. Lopes suspected that the box at Turner Field exceeded this measurement, allowing catchers to set up a little further off the plate and perhaps get more called strikes. If so, this would be an advantage to pitchers like Greg Maddux and Tom Glavine, both of whom often relied on getting borderline strike calls.

As we watched from the broadcast booth, we weren't sure what exactly was being discussed. But as we often do, we asked the TV truck to roll tape, just in case this turned out to be a story.

The next night, it became one. Braves catcher Fernando Lunar was called for a rare catcher's balk, for lining up with one foot out of the catcher's box. Bobby Cox was ejected for arguing the call. While Cox watched and listened from inside the clubhouse, we discussed what we had seen the night before, superimposing the Friday night catcher's box over the Saturday box. The Saturday box was smaller.

We weren't even sure which night's box was the correct size, but among our speculations was the possibility that the Braves had gotten caught bending the rules a bit. There was also the possibility that a simple mistake had been made by the ground crew on one of those nights.

We were simply doing our jobs, trying to report the story as it developed. But the Braves didn't see it that way, and the next day they blamed the messenger. All four broadcasters were told that we would no longer be allowed to fly on the team charter.

This seemed like a strange way to punish us, if that's what they were trying to do. The team was leaving the next day for Montreal and since we weren't allowed on the charter, the team had to buy us commercial airline tickets (all mandated first class by our contracts), pay our cab fare to the hotel, and, when we returned to Atlanta, pay for our airport parking.

We were also told not to leak a word of this to the media, but it was kind of hard for them to miss. When Carroll Rogers of the *Atlanta Journal-Constitution* and Bill Zack of the *Gwinnett Daily News* boarded their flight to Montreal on Monday, there sat Skip, Pete, Don, and Joe.

It didn't take long for them to figure it out.

The front page of the *Atlanta Journal-Constitution* the next day included one of my favorite headlines ever:

Truth Won't Fly On Braves Plane?

Team and station officials met the next day and ironed out the situation. It was over in a day. But since we had received tickets for the entire trip, which also included a three-day stop in New York, we decided to use them.

It took a little time for this whole thing to blow over. Joe Simpson took the most heat, since he happened to be on TV explaining the odd situation when Bobby arrived in the clubhouse after being ejected. Bobby was a little cool toward all of us for a while, but eventually it was forgotten.

It was also expensive. Besides paying additional travel expenses for the four of us, the Braves also paid a hefty fine for the catcher's box infraction—whether intentional or accidental.

We never were really able to find out exactly what happened here. In fact, if you want to have a conversation end quickly, just ask Bobby Cox or any other Braves official about the catcher's box incident in 2000.

The Braves won their ninth consecutive division title that year, but this time they did not make it out of the Division Series. The St. Louis Cardinals swept the series by scores of 7–5, 10–4, and 7–1. Atlanta's starting pitching trio of Maddux, Glavine, and Millwood were all hit hard. None of the three made it past the fifth inning.

But the pitching performance I most remember came from Cardinals opening game starter Rick Ankiel. The 21-year-old southpaw had won 11 games during the regular season for St. Louis. Leading 6–0 going into the third inning, Ankiel suddenly—and, as it turned out, permanently—lost the ability to throw a strike. His third-inning meltdown included four walks and five wild pitches. Ankiel never pitched effectively in the major leagues again, but he did return in 2007 as an outfielder.

* * *

The 2001 season was moving toward another successful finish when the September 11 terrorist attacks occurred. Major League Baseball shut down for a week, and we resumed play on September 17 in Philadelphia. While we were all happy to be back working, like everyone else we were still horrified by what had happened. You couldn't get it off your mind.

After any game at Veterans Stadium in Philadelphia, most of the radio and TV broadcasters for both teams would gather back in the press lounge to kill the time while traffic cleared before the team bus left. The first night back after 9/11, we were there having a beer when Phillies broadcaster Harry Kalas asked everyone to stand and join hands. And Harry, who loved to sing, led us in a chorus of "God Bless America."

When the four-game series ended, we were on our way to New York. As they often did, the TV station ordered a limo for the broadcast crew. As we headed north on the Jersey Turnpike, the ride seemed just like the ones we'd taken so many times before—having a drink, talking about the game, telling stories.

Suddenly, on this trip, all of that stopped. We were closing in on the city, and the shafts of light illuminating the Ground Zero rescue and recovery efforts came into view. You couldn't help but stare and think, "My God, this is where it happened." I don't know if anybody said a word the rest of the way to the hotel.

The next morning, an officer from the NYPD offered us an opportunity to visit Ground Zero. A group of about 20 Braves players, broadcasters, and executives left the Grand Hyatt and took a downtown subway from Grand Central Station to within about 12 blocks of where the Twin Towers once stood. That was as far as you could go. We then began walking toward the ruins, which were still cordoned off.

I could only go so far. There was a fine dust still covering everything. There was an odd odor in the air. And the closer we got, you could see those shards of metal off in the distance. Some of the group proceeded as close as they were allowed to go. But I had seen enough. I turned away after I'd gone just a few blocks and returned to the hotel.

Exiting the subway, you walk through Grand Central Station to get back to the Grand Hyatt. Displayed in Grand Central were pictures of missing persons, and the display was somewhat overwhelming. All races, nationalities, ages, and occupations were represented. There were informal family photos, birthday parties, picnics. There were professional photographs of executive types. It was an entire cross-section of the city.

Pictures like these were posted all over town. You couldn't go anywhere without seeing them. The city was also noticeably quiet. There were cabs everywhere, but nobody was blowing their horn. The streets were full of people, but there didn't seem to be much conversation. It was a city still in shock.

Some streets were inaccessible to traffic to allow rescue and recovery teams to get to and from Ground Zero. Occasionally, you would see a truck full of firemen returning and you couldn't help but notice the expressions on their faces. All you could think was, "This is what it must be like in a war."

Some of the out-of-town rescue workers were staying at our hotel. One fireman from Oklahoma told us about his day. His particular group was working in an area where there had been an underground garage. They found a brass nameplate intact. They wondered where it had come from, and had it checked out. When told that it had been in an office on the 70th or 71st floor, they realized the enormity of what they were dealing with. There were stories like this everywhere you went.

Even once we got to Shea Stadium before the game, the familiar security guards, clubhouse attendants, and press lounge workers each had stories. Almost all of them knew someone who was still missing.

This was the first major professional sporting event in New York City since 9/11. The game itself was preceded by one of the most moving ceremonies I had ever seen. It included police and fire personnel from all five boroughs, a traditional group of bagpipers, and a number of city and state officials including New York mayor Rudy Giuliani.

Braves players were lined up along the third-base line and Mets players along the first-base line for the ceremonies, which ended with a video tribute to those still missing and the national anthem performed live by Diana Ross. When the ceremonies ended, players from each side walked over and hugged each other before returning to their respective dugouts.

When we came back on the air, Don was choked up. "The players are hugging each other," he said. "I've never seen that before."

Throughout the game, Mets players wore the caps representing all branches of the rescue and recovery teams, including the New York City Fire and Police departments and the Port Authority. The night had special significance for Jason Marquis, the Braves starting pitcher that night. A Staten Island native, he had lost several friends and former high school classmates in the collapse of the World Trade Center.

With the game tied 1–1 in the seventh inning, Liza Minnelli went on the field during the seventh-inning stretch to lead the crowd of 41,235 in a chorus of "New York, New York." The Braves took a 2–1 lead in the top of the eighth on a Brian Jordan RBI double. But in the bottom half of the inning, Mike Piazza hit a two-run homer off of reliever Steve Karsay, and the Mets held on to win 3–2.

After what New Yorkers had been through, no one really minded that the Mets won that night. As Tom Glavine said after the game, "There was a higher power at work here tonight."

The Braves held on to win the NL East over the Phillies by two games, but the postseason woes continued. In the Division Series, the Braves once again swept the Houston Astros. They had this part down pat.

Since 1997, they'd played the Astros three times in the NLDS and won nine out of 10 games. But in the National League Championship Series, the combination of Arizona's Randy Johnson and Curt Schilling proved to be too much for Atlanta bats. The Diamondbacks won three straight games in Turner Field to take the series 4–1.

* * *

In 2002, the Braves won 101 games and finished an incredible 19 games ahead of Montreal. But in the Division Series, it was the San Francisco Giants prevailing 3–2. The clincher came in Atlanta on October 7. If the Braves had won that night, we would have flown to St. Louis following the game to play the Cardinals in the NLCS.

Instead, after the loss, we had to go to the loading dock to pick up our luggage, which we had dropped off earlier in the day. After getting my bags, I was walking past the FOX Network TV truck, where a technician was unplugging some cables. Spotting me, he said, "Going home early again, huh?"

"Yeah," I answered, "it's like a bad habit we can't seem to shake."

Chapter 14

Of Mikes and Men

At the end of the 2002 season, I had completed my 27th year as a broadcaster for the Atlanta Braves. And I had never been happier. Not only was I firmly entrenched in my dream job, but I was working for an organization that was now considered one of the best, if not *the* best, in baseball. But what made it really enjoyable were the people with whom I worked.

It all began with Ernie Johnson and Skip Caray. When the three of us began our first year together as Braves broadcasters in 1976, we had no idea if the chemistry was there to make it work or not. We needn't have worried. We meshed immediately.

I got to know Ernie during the three months leading up to the 1976 season by working alongside him helping to sell advertising for the program, yearbook, and radio network. By the time we worked our first game together in spring training, we were already comfortable with each other.

After our introductory press conference in December, I didn't see much of Skip until spring training. We worked our first game together on March 28, 1976, a preseason meeting between the Braves and the Minnesota Twins at Tinker Field in Orlando, Florida.

At some point during that game, Skip was reviewing the managerial career of Twins skipper Gene Mauch.

"You know, Pete," he said. "I keep hearing Gene Mauch being referred to as a great manager. But if you look at his career, this is his 17th year as a big league manager and he's never won a thing."

"And," I replied, "he was at the helm of that 1964 Phillies team that had a 6½ game lead with 12 games left in the season and blew it. The Cardinals won that year."

Skip was impressed that I knew that off the top of my head, and when the commercial break came at the end of that inning, he said, "We're going to be all right together."

And we were—for nearly 33 years.

There was never a question about Ernie. He had been a Braves broadcaster since the team arrived in Atlanta in 1966. In fact, Ernie actually moved to Georgia a year earlier to put together the Braves radio network. He traveled all over the Southeast, signing up stations and laying the groundwork for what is now the largest radio network for any professional sports team in the country, at more than 200 stations strong.

Ernie, of course, was a former pitcher for the Braves, including that 1957 World Championship team. He would always downplay his role for those Milwaukee teams, though.

"I was just a middle reliever," he'd tell you. "Couldn't start, couldn't finish."

But if you look up his record, he had a pretty good major league career. A 40–23 record. A 3.77 ERA. He even hit a home run in 1957.

"I hit it off Steve Ridzik of the Giants," Ernie recalled, "and the next day, the Giants sent him back to the minors."

On the air, he had a folksy style once described by *Atlanta Journal-Constitution* columnist Ron Hudspeth as "comfortable as a pair of old slippers."

Ernie was proud of his Brattleboro, Vermont, roots and even prouder of his wife, Lois, and their family. If an afternoon game went into extra innings, he would often say on the air, "Take the roast out of the oven, Lois. I'm going to be a little late."

Ernie gave me the nickname "The Professor," but not for the reasons you might think. He thought I resembled Jim Brosnan, who pitched for the Cubs, Cardinals, and Reds when Ernie was playing for the Braves. Brosnan was called "The Professor" for his scholarly appearance and because while he was still playing, he wrote a couple of best-selling diary-type books about the game.

The nickname stuck with me because of my knowledge and love of baseball research.

Ernie's easy-going manner on the air was exactly the same off the air. Just a very nice man. If you heard us refer to him as "Uncle Ernie," well, that's what it felt like when you worked with him—just like sitting alongside a kindly uncle.

Skip was a totally different type. Brash, cynical, impatient—these are all words that have been used to describe him. Skip also possessed one of the quickest minds and sharpest wits of anyone I have ever been around.

He had already established himself in Atlanta as the voice of the Atlanta Hawks, and listeners were often treated to his cleverness. Late in a lopsided game, Skip would often say, "If you promise to patronize our sponsors, you have my permission to walk your dog." Bob Costas has called that "the most original line ever uttered by a sportscaster."

Skip also had a mischievous side and loved showing it off. In 1979, I was asked by a neighbor for help securing one of the team mascots for our sub-division's Fourth of July parade. This was a small annual event, the kind where children wear red, white, and blue and decorate their bikes. Skip got wind of it and began talking about it on the air—but began referring to it as the "Famous Chamblee Fourth of July Parade." And he told the nation that I was going to be the parade's Grand Marshal.

Every night, Skip would exaggerate the size and nature of the parade. And every night I would counter by reminding our viewers that this was a simple parade for kids in a local sub-division. But Skip wouldn't let up. Within a week, he had Barry Manilow, the Mormon Tabernacle Choir, the Montreal Canadiens, all surviving original cast members from *Gone With the Wind*, Richard Nixon, and Mr. Twinkie all supposedly scheduled to march in our little parade.

Our neighbor, Suzy Murphy, who was in charge of the parade, became so exasperated that she called renowned *Atlanta Constitution* columnist Lewis Grizzard to see if he could get the newspaper to run a story clarifying the small neighborhood nature of the parade. Well, this was right up Lewis' alley. He wrote a column on the whole situation. The column began:

"This is a crazy story, but when I found out Skip Caray was the cause of it, I understood why."

Once the column appeared, Suzy began getting calls from local TV stations who wanted to come out and cover the parade. She then asked me if I would serve as a sort of Grand Marshal. I did, sitting in a convertible that had a sign attached to the back that said, "Eat your heart out, Skip. Maybe we'll invite you next year."

And Mr. Twinkie, the Hostess bakery mascot, *was* there!

"After Skip kept mentioning Mr. Twinkie," Suzy said, "I felt obliged to invite him—and he accepted."

Skip loved every minute of the entire episode.

* * *

Early one season, when the Braves were off to a terrible start, the *Atlanta Constitution* ran a story on the lack of fan interest in the team. According to the story, no one was going to the games, no one was watching the games on TV, and nobody cared. Skip took exception to this article and on that day's telecast asked viewers to call the newspaper and tell them, "I'm watching the Braves." He repeated this invitation several times, giving out the newspaper's telephone number each time. The volume of calls so overloaded the paper's switchboard that it took nearly a day to get the system up and running again.

On another occasion, Skip had a joke that he wanted to tell on the air. When he told it to us, we flinched.

"I don't know, Skip," Ernie said. "That may be a little too dirty for family television."

But you couldn't tell Skip no. He came up with the idea to just give the punch-line which, by itself, was inoffensive. Thus began the "Punch Line of the Night" routine, which lasted several weeks. Every night Skip would deliver the innocuous punch line to some of the raunchiest jokes on the planet. The fans loved it.

The three of us also discovered that we enjoyed doing things together away from the ballpark. We loved going out to dinner on the road after a day game or having a couple of drinks after a night game.

Ernie and I used to play golf whenever we had a chance, and our contacts in baseball were able to get us on some fabulous courses, including Oakmont, Bellerive, PGA National, and that memorable doubleheader on an off day in California: Pebble Beach in the morning, Spyglass Hill in the afternoon.

During the mid-1980s, Skip decided that he, too, wanted to be part of our golf outings. So during one off-season, he took lessons and by the next season deemed himself ready to give the game a try.

Skip joined Ernie, John Sterling, and me for his first-ever round of golf at the Stardust Country Club in San Diego, sporting a brand new set of clubs, new golf shoes…he was ready! Ernie, John, and I hit our tee shots on the first hole, but Skip kept walking around, eyes lowered, as if he was looking for something.

Ernie finally said, "Go ahead, Skip—hit away."

Skip continued looking around, and then asked, "Where did you get the balls?"

All of his lessons had been on a driving range, where there was always a bucket of balls nearby.

"You don't have any golf balls?" Ernie asked, laughing. "You've got to buy some in the pro shop."

"That's okay," Skip replied. "I'll just use one of yours."

"No-o-o-o," Ernie said, still chuckling. "Go buy some—you'd better get a dozen."

We laughed about that all day.

As it turned out, Skip didn't care much for the game. And after a few months, he gave it up.

If it seems like the three of us spent a lot of time laughing, it's because we did. We truly enjoyed each other's company. Our wives and families became close. It was the perfect working environment. Even when things went awry, we tried to make the best of it. One spring, we had back-to-back broadcasts scheduled at Pompano Beach Municipal Park, the tiny spring training home of the Texas Rangers. Friday was to be radio only, Saturday both radio and TV. There was one problem. The Rangers were also scheduled for a radio broadcast on Saturday and there were only two broadcast booths.

"Don't worry," we were told by TBS executive producer Don Ellis, "we'll build a temporary TV booth on the press box roof for you guys."

Ernie and I worked the Friday game, and throughout the afternoon we could hear the hammering and pounding above us as work proceeded on our temporary working quarters. When the game ended, Ernie and I took a skeptical look at the new booth. It was nothing more than a plywood lean-to, accessible only by climbing a ladder.

Skip joined us the next day, and on our way to the ballpark we joked with him about the set-up. But when we arrived, the booth was gone. A thunderstorm with high winds had rolled through overnight. Our booth didn't make it. The only evidence of it was a couple of ragged strips of plywood lying on the roof.

We wound up broadcasting that game from a pagoda-like structure down the third-base line beyond the grandstand. You could hardly see home plate from there, but we had our TV monitors and gave it our best effort. That was something we always tried to do, and it resulted in more accolades than we ever imagined possible.

We were three different broadcasters with three different personalities and three different styles. But the chemistry and camaraderie were there, and when our games started going across the nation on cable, fans and media critics alike responded.

It was almost impossible to keep up with all of the fan mail we began to receive. The station printed picture postcards of the broadcast team that we could sign and send back as a response.

And as for the media critics, here is just a sampling:

"Is there a better broadcast team than Skip…Pete…and Ernie …? I haven't been exposed to it."

—Ray Kenney, *Milwaukee Journal*, August 11, 1983

"America's broadcast team in easy to take doses…I could listen to these guys all night."

—Larry Bonko, *Virginian-Pilot*, August 14, 1983

"Without a doubt, the team of Johnson, Caray, and Van Wieren…set the standard of excellence to which other broadcasting teams will aspire,"

—Jeff Archer, *Baseball Gold* magazine, October 1983

"America's team is really Skip and Ernie and Pete…"

—Jack Bogaczyk, *Roanoke Times & News World*, September 11, 1983

"The Superstation boasts a top-shelf baseball crew in Ernie…Pete…and Skip…"

—Jerry Trecker, *Hartford Courant*, April 21, 1985

"The best TV broadcast crew in any sport may be working on cable TV at WTBS. Ernie…Pete…and Skip blend so well alternating on TV and radio that you hardly notice when one is replaced by another."

—Howard Rosenberg, *Los Angeles Times*, May 29, 1985

"The best broadcast team in the National League. Ernie…and Pete…are low key but smart, and Skip…can be sarcastically funny."

—David Levine, *SPORT* magazine, July, 1985

"The Braves announcers have fans across the nation."

—Rudy Martzke, *USA Today*, May 22, 1986

When baseball broadcasting historian Curt Smith ranked the game's 101 all-time best announcers in his 2005 book, *Voices of Summer*, all three of us made the list. Ernie was No. 43, Skip No. 45, and I was No. 59. It was such an honor and so much fun to be part of this trio.

When Ernie retired at the end of the 1989 season, we were fortunate to have Don Sutton already on board to step into that slot. Don joined our broadcast team that year after retiring from his Hall of Fame pitching career.

Years earlier, I had interviewed Don at Dodger Stadium for a pregame radio show. When the interview ended, we continued to chat, mostly about broadcasting. When Don stood up to leave, he looked back at me and said, "I'm going to work with you some day." And I'll be darned, in 1989 here he was.

As much as I enjoyed working with Ernie and Skip, I always felt I did my best work when paired with Don. We had an immediate chemistry, always seemed to know where the other person was trying to go, and had genuine admiration and respect for each other.

We also had similar interests away from the booth—golf, music, and restaurants. One of the few things we were never able to agree on was the importance of wine. Don is a wine connoisseur. I am a beer drinker. Many a night, Don would offer me a sip of his latest discovery.

"Here, taste this," he would say. "Do you get the jammy texture, maybe like a blackberry jam?"

I would reply, "Tastes like grapes to me."

"Ahhh," he'd growl. "Drink your Heineken."

* * *

There was no drop-off in the quality of our broadcasts when Don arrived, or when we added Joe Simpson to the mix in 1992. Of course, their arrivals coincided with the team's turnaround, so we had plenty of good things to talk about, which always makes it easier.

And the media critics were just as kind as they had been to Ernie, Skip, and me.

"Skip…Pete…and Don…can't be beat for insight and entertainment."
—Ron Kozlowski, *Palm Beach Post*, August 16, 1991

"These broadcasting pros give TBS a decided edge over rival cable 'Super station' WGN."
—Dusty Saunders, *Rocky Mountain News*, September 2, 1991

And after Joe arrived:

"The likable, refreshingly unslick TBS broadcast crew of Pete…Skip… Don…and Joe is my favorite announcing team. These low-key mavens are not only smart, funny, and chatty, but effortlessly so."

—Howard Rosenberg, *Los Angeles Times*, September 2, 2002

Throughout these 27 years, we were backed by an absolutely top-notch production team. From our producer Glenn Diamond on down, TBS consistently delivered a network-level production each and every day. There was great camaraderie between us and the production crew. We even created an annual bowling tournament—"BOWLERO"—held on an off-day on the road, when we would all get together for a day of fun and relaxation.

A great team on the field…a great team in the booth…a great team in the truck. We had it all working like a well-oiled machine as that 2002 season ended.

But everything took a sudden turn the next year.

Chapter **15**

"We're Losing Our Vin Scullys"

On Monday, March 24, 2003, I drove back to Atlanta from Orlando. With one week remaining until the start of the regular season, I was encouraged by the upbeat atmosphere I had seen in spring training. This Braves team was not hanging their heads over another disappointing postseason in 2002. They seemed more determined than ever to get back there this year and win it all.

Normally, I would have stayed for the final few days of spring training, but our Florida broadcasts were finished and Turner Sports had called a baseball staff meeting for Tuesday. This was highly unusual. We always had a day-long meeting in late January or early February but never anything this close to the season.

Our last January meeting had been a little different. All the usual attendees were there—the broadcasters, producers, directors, statisticians, and other staffers. And the itinerary followed its usual course: showing us the new screen graphics, telling us about sold features that would need to be incorporated into the games, giving us a feel for what the studio show would include and all of the other business matters that need to be gone over before the start of a new season.

But there was a new and added twist this year. Mark Lazarus, who had just been promoted from president of Turner Sports to president of Entertainment Networks (TBS, TNT, etc.) was conducting the meeting. He talked about how ratings had flattened out, and that was certainly true. It had been happening since our peak year, 1983, when the national cable rating for Braves games on TBS was 4.9. By 1993, it had dropped to 2.7. And for the last five years, it had been in the 1.4-1.6 range.

A major reason for the drop was the explosive growth of regional sports networks from Fox and Sportschannel that had blanketed the country. The New York Yankees even had their own channel, the YES Network, to carry Yankees games. The Braves were no longer the only game in town.

While the 2002 number had been 1.4, that was still 20 percent higher than ESPN baseball telecasts and almost 50 percent higher than the baseball ratings on Chicago's WGN, the other Superstation.

"But," Lazarus said, "we need that number to get bigger, and we need the demographics of who is watching to get younger." Lazarus had a sales background, and targeting that 18–49 age group is the *raison d'être* for everyone in TV sales.

He then introduced Steve Rabb, who had recently conducted a focus group study of Braves baseball on TBS. This particular group was based in Indianapolis, and their judgments on our telecasts included the following:

We were too biased toward the Braves. Sometimes we called players by their first name only. It felt like a local broadcast. These and other such opinions followed.

As Rabb read off these items, we announcers kept glancing at each other, no doubt thinking the same things. Of course it felt like a local broadcast—it was. It was also the most successful local team telecast in baseball history. Of course there was some tilt toward the Braves...we were the Braves broadcasters! And as for first names only, sometimes that was required to distinguish one Jones (Chipper) from the other (Andruw). The viewers knew who we meant.

Plus, the mere fact that this focus group was based in Indianapolis made no sense. That's right in the heart of Cincinnati Reds country, so an anti-Braves sentiment was probable.

After this presentation, Lazarus and executive producer Mike Pearl put us on notice that this year's telecasts were to be more neutral and have more of a national feel. Okay, if that's what they wanted, we could do that. I'm not sure our fans would like it, but we could give it a try.

Now they were having us back in March for another meeting. Normally, whenever we attended a meeting at Turner Sports headquarters, the routine was the same. You would get off the elevator on the 13th floor of the CNN Center's North Tower and check at the switchboard to find out which conference room to go to. If you were early, you might wander the halls, sticking your head in an office or two to say hello to folks you hadn't seen in awhile. Eventually, you would head to the appropriate meeting room. It was all very informal.

But on this day—Tuesday, March 25—Mike Pearl's secretary, Ann, was waiting when the elevator doors opened to escort me straight to Mr. Pearl's office. Once I was in the office, Ann left, closing the door. It was just the two of us, Mike and me.

"Where are the rest of the guys?" I asked.

"We're meeting with everyone separately today," Pearl responded. "Have a seat."

After some small talk about spring training, Pearl got to the purpose of the meeting.

"We have decided," he began, "to make a change in the broadcast pairings this year."

"Okay."

He continued, "We are going to reunite you with your original partner (meaning Skip), and you two will do the 36 games on SportSouth (our regional network). Don and Joe will be the broadcast team for the 90 TBS games. You and Skip will work those games on radio."

I was stunned by this decision.

"Have you told Skip yet?" I asked.

"Yes, he was in earlier."

"What did he say about this?"

With that, Pearl turned and called up a screen on his computer. He had apparently entered Skip's response right after Skip left.

"Let's see," said Pearl. "He said, 'Run that by me again…I like working with Pete, that's no problem…Can you tell me why we're doing this?'"

"That was about to be my next question," I said.

Pearl then went on to explain the new concept of calling the broadcasts "MLB on TBS" and how we were too closely associated with the Braves.

"But these are all Braves telecasts, are they not?" I asked.

"Yes, it's the same schedule, but we are going to try this new approach."

"Well…all right," I said. I'm sure he could hear the disappointment in my voice.

Pearl then called vice president of public relations Greg Hughes into the office. Greg walked me down the hall to his office, closed the door and began some idle conversation that lasted for about 10-15 minutes. I felt like I was at a debriefing. Then his phone rang, he answered and said only, "Okay. Thank you." And then to me he said, "Come on, I'll walk you to the elevator."

As we walked down a different hallway than the one where I had come in, it dawned on me: *I know what this is. They've got one of the other guys in there now. They just want to make sure we don't run into each other while we're here. That is pretty weak.*

My thoughts were spinning as I exited the building and drove home. This was going to be tough news to break to my family. When I told Elaine, she had a better sense than I did of what would happen.

"That'll never work," she said. "The fans are going to be very upset."

Skip made a similar statement when he called that night. At first, we swapped jokes about what we were going to do with all of our TBS-branded golf shirts, which we would no longer need. We compared notes over what we had been told. Then Skip said, "It's not going to work…but in the meantime, I'll see you on the radio."

The next day the news broke that Skip and I were out at TBS. Almost immediately, I received a call from team president Stan Kasten.

"I just want you to know," he said, "that we [the Braves] had nothing to do with this."

Bobby Cox found out what had happened in Vero Beach, Florida, where the Braves were about to play the Dodgers. His response to *Atlanta*

Journal-Constitution writer Dave O'Brien was "That's ridiculous. I'm completely shocked! We're losing our Vin Scullys."

Bobby told us later that he was reprimanded by team officials after making these remarks. "This is a television issue," he was told. "Stay out of it." But we knew he was outraged by what had happened, as were many others employed by the Braves. Their support meant a lot to both of us.

When the local media called, Skip and I tried to stay positive. Skip told the *Atlanta Journal-Constitution*'s Tim Tucker, "Am I disappointed? Yes. Was I shocked? Yes. Is it something to sulk about? Absolutely not. I'm lucky. I'm working with Pete and doing a lot of radio. Who can complain? I can't."

My words to Tim were similar: "I'll prepare the same and give the same effort that I always have. My schedule hasn't changed. My income hasn't changed. All that changes is I go to a different booth. The people who run the station have the right to make whatever decision they want to make. And we move on."

When the news began to reach the fans, the outcry was immediate and strong. In an online poll, they posed the question, "Do you like the Braves' juggling of their TV announcers?" On the first night alone, they received more than 11,000 responses. The results: No, it's horrible—9,902 (89%); Yes, it's great—1,245 (11%).

* * *

Our first game after this came on Friday night at Turner Field, one of the final preseason games of the spring against Baltimore. It was very awkward for all of us.

While I was filling out my scorebook in the radio booth, a young man came in, handed me a business card and introduced himself. It was Jeff Pomeroy, newly hired by the Turner Sports public relations department.

"We are asking all of you guys to refer any questions you get about this to either Greg Hughes or myself," he said. "We'll both be up here all night. Okay?"

"If that's what you want," I answered.

"Okay," Pomeroy said. "Thanks, Joe. Can you tell me where I can find Pete?"

I tried to remain calm.

"I'm Pete," I explained. "This is the radio booth. If you are looking for Joe, you might find him in the TV booth next door."

The red-faced newcomer left quickly.

I said nothing more. But our radio producer, Dave Baker, who witnessed the exchange, must have seen the steam coming from my ears.

"Geez, Pete," Dave said. "Who are these people?"

The groundswell of support for Skip and me continued to grow as the season began. Much of it was documented by then *Atlanta Journal-Constitution* sports media columnist Mike Tierney. On March 30, Tierney reported that the ajc.com poll now had more than 20,000 respondents, with 92 percent calling the move "horrible."

Elsewhere online, petitions were popping up to "Bring back Skip and Pete." Paper petitions were making their way through the stands at Turner Field. Skip and I could not get away from it. Every three days or so, a new team would come to Atlanta, or we'd go to a new city and have to explain what had happened all over again.

It is a short walk from the media parking lot at Turner Field to the media entrance, but every day there would be a cluster of fans waiting for us, asking what they could do to get us back on TBS. Meanwhile, the station and the team were being bombarded with emails, telephone calls, and letters demanding our return.

TBS executives were making it even worse with some of their comments.

"We need to maintain a vibrancy to the telecast," Lazarus told Tierney in the *Atlanta Journal-Constitution*.

Pearl explained the move to SI.com's John Donovan by saying, "We've been squeezing this same orange for an awfully long time."

To add to the initial hurt, we were now being humiliated and insulted by these executives.

Then the national media began chiming in.

"The reformulation rightfully is drawing comparisons to New Coke. Skip Caray was entertaining and always told the truth. Van Wieren? Pure professional."

—Fritz Quindt, *The Sporting News*, April 21, 2003

"A 63-year-old man (Caray) is being pushed aside after decades of loyal service.... But the real victim here is Van Wieren, who has long been the best and most professional part of the Braves' broadcast."

—Scott Zucker, *USA Today Baseball Weekly*, April 15, 2003

Try as we might to just carry on and do our jobs, this just wouldn't go away. In fact, the intensity grew as the season progressed. Newspaper columns, fan petitions, letters, emails, phone calls—the barrage continued.

And as for the new MLB on TBS concept? The ratings had taken a tumble—down 29 percent. We were now finishing behind ESPN on head-to-head nights. ESPN Senior Producer Tim Scanlan was in Atlanta for one of their Sunday night broadcasts and stopped me in the walkway to the press box.

"I don't know why they took you and Skip off the air," he said, "but it's really been good for us."

How did TBS ever get itself into such a predicament?

Several years later, someone who was close to the situation told me his version of what had happened. Since no one that I've told this to has ever disputed it, I've got to believe that there is at least some truth to it. Here's what I was told:

The idea originated with Mike Pearl, normally an extremely competent executive producer, who won numerous Emmys for his work. When the proposal was made, Pearl, Steve Rabb, and production services manager Bill Callen were all for it. Greg Hughes, Braves producer Glenn Diamond, and baseball studio producer Tim Kiely were opposed. Mark Lazarus wasn't leaning strongly one way or the other, but when the decision was made to go with the new plan, he and his successor, David Levy, became supporters.

By June, the furor still had not diminished—and many of those who created it were gone. Lazarus had exited sports for his new position overseeing the entertainment networks. Pearl had resigned to return to ABC-TV. Rabb left the company to conduct his "focus groups" elsewhere.

Finally, David Levy, the new sports president, decided to act. He scheduled a meeting for Monday, July 7, in his New York office. The Braves were in New York that day to open a series with the Mets. Attending the meeting with Levy were the four broadcasters, plus Glenn Diamond, Greg Hughes, and Jeff Behnke, who had succeeded Pearl as executive producer.

Once assembled, Levy told us that after the All-Star break (July 17), we would be returning to our four-man rotation. As happy as I was to hear the news, I was somewhat irritated that there were no apologies offered to Skip and me for the insult and humiliation this whole situation had caused. In fact, much of the meeting was spent listening to Levy describe all of the responsibility he had as both Turner Sports president and director of international sales for Turner Broadcasting.

When the meeting adjourned, Skip and I began walking back to our hotel. About halfway there, Skip said to me, "You know, I don't even care about being back on TV—I like radio so much better. But you know what I do care about?"

"What's that?" I asked.

Holding up his right hand to give me a high five, Skip replied, "We beat those bastards!"

Back in Atlanta, our return was top of the front page news in the *Atlanta Journal-Constitution*. Tim Tucker's story quoted David Levy:

"Ultimately, the fans have spoken, and we have listened."

"It's nice to be back," Skip said. "The public support was humbling."

My words to Tim: "The fans are the ones that made this happen, and I'll never forget that."

I never have.

Chapter **16**

End of an Era

While all of this was going on, the Braves were rolling along toward a 12th consecutive division title. Again, they did so with relative ease, clinching the division with two weeks remaining in the season and winning by a comfortable 10-game margin over the second-place Florida Marlins.

This was one of the most complete teams Atlanta had during its division title run. The Braves led the National League in batting average (.284) and home runs (235). The lineup featured a veritable "Murderers' Row" of Gary Sheffield (.330, 39 HR, 132 RBIs), Javy Lopez (.328, 43, 109), Andruw Jones (.277, 36, 116), and Chipper Jones (.305, 27, 106).

On the pitching side, Tom Glavine had departed and signed with the New York Mets. But the Braves acquired Russ Ortiz in a trade with the Giants, and the newcomer won 21 games. Greg Maddux, Mike Hampton, Horacio Ramirez, and Shane Reynolds also posted double-digit win totals, Maddux for a major league record 16th consecutive season. The bullpen was anchored by John Smoltz, who recorded 45 saves.

Despite all of this firepower, Atlanta went out in the first playoff round again, losing the Division Series to the Chicago Cubs, three games to two. The Cubs' one-two pitching punch of Kerry Wood and Mark Prior silenced Atlanta bats in the three Chicago victories. The Braves scored just 15 runs and hit just .215 for the series.

With Glavine already gone, Greg Maddux was the next to leave, becoming a free agent and signing with the Cubs after the 2003 season.

A storied era for Atlanta pitching was gradually ending. Leo Mazzone had been the pitching coach for Atlanta ever since Bobby Cox returned to the field in 1990. He had worked wonders resuscitating the careers of pitchers such as John Burkett and Mike Remlinger. But even Leo admitted, "It's a pretty easy job when you have pitchers named Greg Maddux, Tom Glavine, and John Smoltz."

But in 2004, Mazzone worked some more of his magic, coaxing 15 wins from newcomer Jaret Wright. Wright had won only 37 games in seven injury-plagued seasons before 2004, and he would win only 16 more over a three-year span after leaving Atlanta following the 2004 season.

Another newcomer, J.D. Drew, led the offense, hitting .305 with 31 home runs and 93 RBIs as the Braves won an unprecedented 13th consecutive division crown. For the fourth time since 1997, they drew the Houston Astros as their Division Series opponent.

The "Killer Bees" now consisted of Bagwell, Biggio, Lance Berkman, and Carlos Beltran. This time the Astros prevailed as all four sparkled, with Beltran having one of the most spectacular Division Series performances ever. For the series, Beltran hit .455 (10-for-22) with four home runs and nine RBIs. He almost single-handedly beat the Braves in the decisive Game 5 with a four-hit, five-RBI performance that included two long home runs. The Astros had finally figured out how to beat the Braves in a Division Series, and Atlanta was out after the first playoff round again.

During spring training prior to that 2004 season, I was standing next to the batting cage one day in Orlando when I heard my name called. Terry McGuirk, the team president, was standing near our dugout and said, "Pete, could you come here? I need to see you for a minute."

I walked over to Terry, who I had known since 1976.

"Yeah, sure," I said. "What's up?"

"You know we have the Braves' Hall of Fame induction ceremony every year," he said.

I certainly did. I had emceed the event for the past three years.

"Well, this year it's going to be on August 13," Terry continued.

I thought he would ask me next if I would be able to emcee the event again. Instead, Terry said, "We would like you to attend this year's event…as an inductee. Both you and Skip have been selected."

My look of surprise brought a smile to Terry's face. He extended his right hand, shook mine, and said, "Congratulations."

What a tremendous feeling that was. Talk about going from the outhouse to the penthouse! A year earlier, Skip and I were being booted off the telecasts, and now we were to receive the highest honor that the Braves could bestow.

As August 13 neared, I could still hardly believe it was happening. I kept looking at the list of names on the Braves Hall of Fame roster: Hank Aaron. Warren Spahn. Eddie Mathews. Phil Niekro. Dale Murphy. Ted Turner, and more. Ernie Johnson had been inducted three years earlier, and now Skip and I would be joining him.

As I prepared my acceptance speech, I struggled with the portion dealing with TBS. I wanted to thank them for the wonderful opportunity they had given me, but I didn't want to include those responsible for the 2003 announcer debacle. I finally settled on this:

"I would like to thank Ted Turner and Terry McGuirk for their leadership, their friendship, and their loyalty. I have worked for eleven different executive producers over the years. I would like to thank ten of them."

I concluded my remarks by recalling a postgame TV interview we had once done with Chipper Jones after he had hit a walk-off game-winning home run against the New York Mets:

"Chipper said, 'Words can't describe it. I just wish everyone could experience such a moment just so they could know how it feels.' Well, Chipper, now I know. Now I know."

That day remains one of the most memorable of my life. It still seems unreal to me whenever I walk the club level concourse at Turner Field and see my portrait hanging there with all of the other Hall of Famers.

* * *

The next year, 2005, was much like so many of the others. The race was a little tighter, but the Braves took over first place on July 22 and never relinquished it, winning the division by two games over the Phillies.

For the 14th consecutive time, we were headed to postseason play, and once again the first-round opponent would be the Houston Astros. Some new faces had arrived on the scene. Catcher Brian McCann and outfielder Jeff Francoeur, both Atlanta natives, were mid-season call-ups and contributed down the stretch. Pitcher Tim Hudson came over in a trade with Oakland and won 14 games.

But the biggest contributions came from a couple of familiar faces.

Andruw Jones had his most productive year ever, hitting 51 home runs and driving in 128. John Smoltz moved back to the starting rotation after four seasons as the closer and went 14–7 with a 3.06 ERA.

In the Division Series, the Astros prevailed three games to one. The final game of that series was an extremely heart-wrenching loss for Atlanta. Leading 6–1 in the bottom of the eighth at Minute Maid Park in Houston, Kyle Farnsworth gave up a grand slam home run to Lance Berkman to make it a one-run game. Farnsworth then surrendered a game-tying solo shot to Brad Ausmus in the bottom of the ninth.

The two teams then battled for nine more innings before Astros utility man Chris Burke won it in the bottom of the eighteenth with a solo homer. It came off Braves reliever Joey Devine, Atlanta's first-round pick in that year's June draft. The Braves didn't know it then, but their 14-year string of consecutive postseason appearances had ended.

It also marked the end of an era in Braves broadcasting. Since 1976, when Ted Turner bought the team, the broadcasts—both on radio and TV—had been under the Turner umbrella. Most of the games were on TBS. Many of those that weren't were carried by SportSouth, a Turner-owned regional sports channel that was later renamed Turner South. All of the games were on the Braves radio network.

As broadcasters, we would rotate freely back and forth between radio and TV, following a schedule put together by the broadcast office at Turner Sports. But now, Time Warner was beginning to sell off parts of the company, and one of the first to go was Turner South, which was purchased by Fox Cable Networks for $375 million. The team was also for sale.

One month into the 2006 season, Fox took control of that 58-game portion of the television schedule. They would be using their own announcers. That left only the 70-game TBS schedule for us to broadcast.

A year earlier, we had added a fifth broadcaster to the mix. Because of some health issues, Skip wanted to cut back on his travel. He lobbied hard for the company to hire his son, Chip, who was ending a seven-year association with the Chicago Cubs in 2004. They did so.

But now, we had fewer games to work and one more broadcaster. As early as April 29, there was speculation in the *Atlanta Journal-Constitution* by Guy Curtright. "TBS will face personnel decisions after this season. Five broadcasters are more than needed to cover 70 TBS telecasts—a number that goes down to 45 in 2008—and 162 radio games."

We all tried not to think about it as the year progressed, and we received virtually no information on what might happen. Then in July came the news that TBS and Fox had signed a $3 billion, seven-year deal with Major League Baseball for the rights to postseason games beginning in 2007. As part of the deal, TBS was given a Sunday Game of the Week, commencing in 2008. The Braves, once the bell-cow of TBS programming, were becoming more and more of a minor presence.

While all of this was going on, the team on the field was struggling.

By the All-Star break, the Braves were 13 games behind the New York Mets, and this year they would not recover. They finished in third place, four games under .500, 18 games behind the Mets. They were out of the postseason mix for the first time since 1990.

Meanwhile, we were all wondering what was going to happen with our overcrowded broadcast booth. Unlike previous administrations, this group communicated almost nothing to us. Previous Turner Sports presidents were often at the ballpark, some on a nightly basis. They would answer any questions we might have, update us on any pertinent issues, or just drop by to say hello. David Levy lived in New York. He didn't even come to see us when we were in New York to play the Mets or Yankees.

Don Sutton suspected that he would be the odd man out since his contract was expiring. He had a home in Atlanta that he wanted to put on the market if that was going to be the case. About a week before leaving for his winter home in California, Don tried to get an answer on his future but was told no decision had been made.

A week later, while waiting to board his plane in Atlanta, he received a call from Jeff Behnke informing him that a new contract would not be offered. Don called me right away with the news. I was furious. He was a good friend, and I was sorry to see him let go.

Don had done excellent work here for 18 years. He had asked for nothing more than the benefit of a few days notice if they were not bringing him back. But they put him off and put him off, then told him by telephone on the day they knew he was leaving for his California home.

In December 2006, we learned that the sale of the Braves was imminent. Liberty Media would be purchasing the club as soon as contract language was finalized and MLB approved the sale. This meant that the radio side of the broadcasts would be moving away from Turner control. What would that mean for the broadcasters? Again, information was difficult to track down.

In early December, I received a call from Jeff Behnke on another matter. While I had him on the line, I asked, "When the sale is approved, will I be working for you or the Braves?"

"The Braves," he answered.

That meant that I was out of the TV mix, as well.

This didn't bother me all that much. Like most baseball broadcasters, I preferred radio, where it's just you and the listeners. This was not like the 2003 situation. The Turner baseball family was splitting up. There were now two television rights-holders—radio would be under the control of the team—and the team itself would have a new owner. It was uncomfortable for everyone, as it always is when a family breaks up. But it certainly could have been handled in a classier, more professional way.

Even their choice of words in releasing the news was maddening. Jeff Pomeroy, speaking for Turner Sports, told the *Atlanta Journal-Constitution*, "Pete's a Braves employee. We've already disposed of his contract."

In 2007, the announcement came that the Braves and TBS would be parting ways at the end of the season. TBS had its new national contract, and the Braves were no longer owned by Time Warner. Games scheduled to be broadcast on TBS would be moved to a new regional version of the station called Peachtree TV.

Thus ended more than 30 years of Atlanta Braves baseball on national cable TV. It had been a long and glorious ride. When our games began showing up on the Superstation back in the '70s, baseball commissioner Bowie Kuhn threatened to use the "best interests of baseball" clause to get them off the air. Thirty years later, commissioner Bud Selig said, "Many thought it would be the death knell of our sport. In fact, Ted Turner helped the sport. His enlightened television policy didn't hurt anything at all. He played a great role in the maturing of the relationship between television and MLB."

It was also the first year of the TBS deal to televise postseason games. There was an assumption made by many that they would use us on those broadcasts. *USA Today* ran several articles mentioning Skip, Joe, and myself as probables for these games. Chip had already been assured a spot.

Whenever ESPN was televising a Braves game, their announcers and their top-notch statistician, Marty Aronoff, would ask, "Do you know yet which series you will be doing?"

Even our own people, Glenn Diamond and Hal Gaalema, another outstanding stats man, were asking, "Has anybody contacted you yet about postseason?"

To all of them, I had to answer, "I've heard nothing."

Finally, in late August, when the Braves were in Cincinnati, Jeff Behnke called. He wanted to do a special on the Braves' long history on TBS. Skip had turned him down, but he still wanted me to be a part of it.

"We can't do it if Skip won't be a part of it," I said. "That just wouldn't make sense."

We talked back and forth for a few more minutes, and he finally agreed that if Skip wouldn't participate, we had no show.

When the subject of the postseason came up, I told Jeff my first obligation was the Braves, who at the time were just six games off the division lead. I was one of their radio voices, and if the Braves made it to postseason, that was where I had to be.

He never officially offered me a postseason slot, but he said several times, "We can't use Skip." Skip's health issues had led to some uneven performances. On most games he was his old self, but occasionally he would have a tough night.

The conversation was amiable, but nothing came out of it.

When the Braves were close to being eliminated in September, again the questions started about my involvement in the postseason coverage. And again, I had no answers for these questions.

Jeff called again after the announcer teams had been named.

"I hope you understand," he said, "but we just couldn't use Skip."

It made me wonder. Am I being bypassed because they didn't want to upset Skip? If so, that was fine with me, but I hoped that wasn't the reason. Skip was upset anyway, and he vented his anger to Tim Tucker of the *Atlanta Journal-Constitution*:

"No one has given me a reason why. I've done a lot of good work for these people and it's hurtful that they apparently don't think I can do good work anymore. I'd like to be voted into the Hall of Fame someday. But when your own employer says you're not good enough to do the playoffs, I don't think that helps your chances."

It was a confusing and awkward time for all of us.

Chapter **17**

The Final Year

As the 2008 season approached, I was leaning more and more toward working one more season then retiring. But before making such a significant decision, I wanted to take an inventory of all of the things I would miss if I took this step.

One of them, I knew, would be the ballparks themselves. I am, and always have been, a ballpark "junkie." I love going to ballparks—big ones, small ones, new ones, old ones. There doesn't even have to be a game going on. If I'm in a town where there's a ballpark I've never been to, I like to stop in and just look around, recall whatever history I know of the place, and just soak in the atmosphere.

Today's new stadiums resemble theme parks with all of their fan plazas, arcade games, face-painting booths, etc. If you get to the park early, there is plenty to do. When I started out, the only pregame activities, outside of batting practice, were events planned by the team that took place on the field.

After Ted Turner bought the Braves in 1976, he was seeking ways to increase attendance, and his last-place team was not getting it done. Enter Bob Hope, the Braves' public relations director. Bob had a fertile imagination for wacky promotions and we, as broadcasters, were involved in a number of them.

On July 26, 1976, Ernie, Skip, and I joined Ted, *Atlanta Journal-Constitution* sportswriter Frank Hyland, and local deejay "Skinny Bobby" Harper in a pregame ostrich race. The team had ordered racing silks for each of us with nicknames on the back. My colors were red and blue, my nickname "Pistol Pete." We sat in sulkies similar to those used in harness racing.

The ostriches pulling the sulkies took off as soon as their handlers released them. To make them turn, you used a broom. Hold the broom beside the bird's right eye and he would turn left, and vice-versa.

When we asked how to stop them, we were told, "Don't worry. They are trained to run to the truck [which was parked behind home plate]—that's where their food is."

So, off we went and let me tell you, those birds can move. When they completed their circuit of the stadium, all of them did run straight to the truck and stop. All but mine. He (or was it a she?) circled home plate and continued running up the first-base line. I didn't know what to do. Hollering "Whoa, whoa, whoa!" didn't work. Finally, the handlers corralled the bird halfway up the right-field line, and I jumped off the sulky.

Pregame promotions such as this were commonplace. Two others that I remember were a frog-jumping contest in which my frog out-leaped those given to Braves players Barry Bonnell and Jerry Royster—and a cow-chip throwing contest that I also won. (Tip: throw them like a Frisbee, not a discus.)

It all worked. Even though the Braves finished in last place in both 1976 and '77, attendance was up in both years. Today's marketing approaches are very different. Pregame entertainment takes place out on the concourses or, if you are in your seats, on humongous video screens.

So what is my favorite ballpark? Here is my criteria as a broadcaster for stadium excellence:

1. The look and feel of the ballpark.
2. The size and location of the broadcast booth. Spacious accommodations, not too high up are preferred.
3. Press lounge food and service. Over the course of a season, you wind up eating more meals there than anywhere else.
4. Clubhouse and press box accessibility. How long does it take to get to either one from the broadcast booth? The shorter the distance, the better.
5. Proximity of the nearest restroom to the broadcast booth. Need I say more? Most commercial breaks last only 90 seconds.

With that in mind, here are my five favorite and least-favorite ballparks.

FAVORITES

1. Fenway Park, Boston—I love everything about this place, the history, plenty of room to work, great food, always an enjoyable experience.

2. Citizen's Bank Park, Philadelphia—The best media setup in the major leagues. Everything you need is close, and the food is terrific.

3. Progressive Field (formerly Jacobs Field), Cleveland—I haven't been there that often, but I love the look and feel of the place, big booths, wide variety of food, plus plenty of pleasant memories from the 1995 World Series.

4. Yankee Stadium (the old one)—Doesn't really meet all of the criteria listed above, but there is *nothing* like a World Series game in this historic place. When the crowd really gets into it, you could actually feel the broadcast booth shake.

5. The two Los Angeles ballparks—I have to declare a dead heat for fifth between Dodger Stadium and Angel Stadium. Dodger Stadium still looks and feels brand new. Angel Stadium has the best broadcast location in the major leagues, low and close to the field.

LEAST FAVORITES

1. Shea Stadium, New York—No contest. Small, dirty booths, world's slowest press elevator, plus the ever-present roar of planes taking off from nearby LaGuardia Airport.

2. Wrigley Field, Chicago—Sorry, traditionalists. This may be a great experience if you are a fan, but it's a tough place to work. Extremely cramped broadcast booths for visiting teams.

3. Olympic Stadium, Montreal—Working conditions weren't bad, but the food was odd, and you always felt like the game was being played inside of a football.

4. Candlestick Park, San Francisco—The booths were all right, but the cold and windy weather made for many an uncomfortable day or night. Also, the press lounge and nearest restroom were a good distance away.

5.   RFK Stadium, Washington—Booths were fine—if you could find them. You had to wend your way through stairwells, offices, and catwalks on various levels to get to them. The new Nationals Park is an improvement, but the booths there are too high, located above the top of some of the light towers.

But even looking at that list of my least favorites, I would still rather have been in any one of them than sitting in an office somewhere.

* * *

My retirement would also eliminate the possibility for any more of those goofy, unpredictable moments that are bound to occur over the course of a broadcast year. One of the most unusual occurred in 1992 on a Saturday night in June at Atlanta-Fulton County Stadium.

We used to get dozens of notes from fans, who sent them up to the TV booth hoping we would mention their names on the telecast. We couldn't mention them all, but every now and then one would catch our attention and on this night, one did. It was from a Tim Kaminski from Tomahawk, Wisconsin.

Don Sutton and I wondered aloud if there really was such a place or if Tim invented the name to get a mention on the air. We quickly found out. Within an hour, the Braves received 81 phone calls and six faxes letting us know that, indeed, there was such a place.

"With a name like Tomahawk," I said, "if the Braves had such a thing as a sister city, that would have to be it. Wouldn't it?"

"Well, maybe," Don replied. "But there might be a few other places out there that would like a designation like that."

"Well, let's find out," I said. "Let's have a contest. Viewers, if you think your hometown should be the Braves' sister city, send us a note and tell us why and we'll pick a winner."

"What will that winner receive?" Don asked.

"I will personally travel there to make it official," I answered.

What a can of worms that opened!

First of all, the response by the viewers was unbelievable. We received 871 entries from 214 cities in 42 states. Some were simple letters, some were accompanied by photos or Chamber of Commerce brochures. The city of New Bern, North Carolina, sent a videotape with local leaders presenting the case for their city.

We also heard from team attorneys, who were concerned with what the Braves' obligation would be to the winner of our little "contest." It seems the FCC has very strict rules and regulations for any over-the-air contests and our spur-of-the-moment game left a host of gray areas. How could we extricate ourselves from this predicament?

We finally decided to declare every city that entered a co-winner.

Certificates declaring each place "An Unofficial Sister City to the Atlanta Braves" were printed up and mailed to all but one place. To keep my end of the bargain, I would deliver the winning certificate to Tomahawk, Wisconsin, in person.

On July 13, an off-day prior to a series at Wrigley Field, our producer, Glenn Diamond, and I flew to Rhinelander, Wisconsin, where we were greeted by Tomahawk officials and driven by motorhome to that picturesque Northern Wisconsin community.

There they had rolled out the red carpet for us.

The first stop was Memorial Park on the shores of Lake Mohawksin, where city and state officials presented us with proclamations and other mementos in front of a large crowd that had assembled to greet us. We were then taken on tours of local businesses—a Harley-Davidson plant, a cardboard box manufacturer, and a wharf where many pleasure boats were docked. The people couldn't have been nicer.

Years later, one of our Braves scouts, Stu Cann, who covers that part of the country, told me that people in Tomahawk were still talking about the day the Braves broadcaster came to their town. I may not have known what I was getting into when I called for the contest, but I'm sure glad I made that trip to Tomahawk. And if they want to call themselves the Braves' "Sister City," it's okay with me.

Aside from the ballparks and those occasional quirky adventures, I knew the things I would miss most if I retired were the games and the people. When you are with a major league team from March to October, the game becomes your second home, and its people are your second family. You are with them seemingly all of the time, and it leads to some very special relationships.

One routine I will always cherish is that morning cup of coffee on the road with manager Bobby Cox. Just about every morning, when I went down to the hotel lobby to get some coffee, there would be Bobby, sometimes alone, sometimes with a couple of coaches or other staff members. We would sit and talk about the previous night's game, other games, items in the news, or whatever subject came up.

Bobby was much more candid during these moments than he would be at the ballpark. He trusted me not to repeat some of the things he said about players, and I never violated that trust. Everything we talked about, both on and off the record, helped me as a broadcaster. It was information that would be hard to get any other way.

Every manager is different. Joe Torre used to treat the broadcasters and his coaches to dinner on the road about once a month. We always looked forward to these get-togethers with Joe, Bob Gibson, Rube Walker, Joe Pignatano, and the broadcast crew. The baseball stories were wonderful and the laughs plentiful as long as you didn't mention Bobby Thomson's "Shot Heard 'Round the World." Rube was the Dodgers' catcher on that day back in 1951 and still bristled whenever the subject was raised.

Chuck Tanner, on the other hand, we hardly ever saw, except at the ballpark. He had three coaches, Bob Skinner, Al Monchak, and Tony Bartirome, who had been with him throughout most of his managerial career, and Chuck spent his time away from the park almost exclusively with them.

You also become at least acquainted with every player who passes through. Some become lifelong friends. For me, that list would include Phil Niekro, Bruce Benedict, Darrell Chaney, Gene Garber, Bob Horner, Mark Lemke, Ron Gant, Brian Jordan, David Justice, Dale Murphy, and, of course, the pitching trio of Maddux, Glavine, and Smoltz.

Having watched those three pitch during all of their Atlanta years was a privilege. They will all be in the Hall of Fame one day, and deservedly so. But whenever I'm asked about the best-pitched games I ever saw, I have a hard time not choosing back-to-back games that were pitched against the Braves in 2004.

On May 16 of that year in Milwaukee, Ben Sheets threw a three-hitter against Atlanta and struck out a club-record 18 in a 4–1 Brewers win.

After an off day, the Braves were back at Turner Field to face Arizona, and in the first game of that series, Randy Johnson pitched a perfect game against the Braves, striking out 13. I can't remember seeing any pitchers with better stuff than Sheets and Johnson had on those two days.

You also get to know players, managers, executives, writers, and broadcasters from other teams. By my count, I have met 79 current Hall of Famers, done pregame shows with 33 of them, and worked at least one game with nine of them. I bring this up not to brag, but because the number should be higher. It is time to forgive Pete Rose and give him his proper due in Cooperstown. Even if the plaque includes a reference to his gambling suspension, Rose belongs.

Some of the people you meet when you travel with a team have nothing to do with the games you're covering. Stop down at the hotel bar after a game, and there's no telling who you might run into.

We've spent evenings chatting with Mike Love, Alan Jardine, and Carl Wilson of the Beach Boys, singer Jerry Vale, Bobby Hatfield of the Righteous Brothers, Penny Marshall, Suzanne Somers, Doc Severinsen, Tommy Smothers, Stevie Nicks, Brian Setzer, and a host of sports figures ranging from Archie Manning to Charles Barkley to Mickey Mantle.

One of the more interesting evenings came the night we met Doc Severinsen, who had been performing with the Milwaukee Symphony Orchestra. He kept us enthralled for a couple of hours with stories from his years as bandleader on *The Tonight Show Starring Johnny Carson.*

But most of the time, you are with your broadcast partners, and that camaraderie is something that I knew I would miss. We always had a good time, both on the air and off. Sometimes, the funny stories just wrote themselves.

One year, after a day game in Pittsburgh, Skip and I were at the hotel bar having a drink, waiting for Ernie. The three of us were headed out to dinner. The fourth member of our crew, John Sterling, walked in with some friends and sat down on the opposite side of the bar. When he noticed us, he said to the bartender, "I'd like to buy those clowns over there a drink."

What he didn't know and couldn't see was—seated behind us and a little bit around a corner were two tables full of…clowns. Nine or ten of them. They had just finished marching in a Shriner's parade and were still in full costume. The bartender followed John's instructions…literally. You should have seen the look on John's face when he was presented with the tab for that round of drinks.

These are the kind of moments that I knew I would really miss as much as the games.

* * *

The 2008 season was not a good one for the Braves. What looked like a pretty good pitching staff when the season opened quickly fell apart.

John Smoltz, Tom Glavine (back with Atlanta after a five-year stint with the New York Mets), Tim Hudson, and relievers Peter Moylan and Rafael Soriano all went down with season-ending injuries.

There were some bright spots offensively. Chipper Jones won his first National League batting title, hitting .364. Brian McCann had another All-Star year (.301, 23 homers, 87 RBIs). And Martin Prado showed promise, hitting .320 in a utility role.

But the Braves couldn't overcome their pitching woes. By the All-Star break, they were six games under .500 and 6½ games behind the division-leading Phillies. Things didn't improve after the break, and by August 2, they were 50–60 and 10 games behind.

Then on August 3, they suffered the most unexpected loss imaginable.

Chapter **18**

Losing a Friend,
a Partner, a Legend

On a June weekend in 2002, the Braves were in Boston for an inter-league series with the Red Sox. The series began on a Friday night with a 4–2 win for Atlanta. It extended the Braves' lead in the National League East to 6½ games over the Montreal Expos. It was a happy bus ride back to the team hotel.

The next game in the series was a Saturday afternoon contest to be televised nationally by Fox. Skip and I had the Braves radio assignment for the day. That morning, I was standing in the hotel motor lobby, awaiting the team bus. I was chatting with a couple of Braves season-ticket holders who had come up to Boston for the series.

Suddenly, one of them, with a look of dismay, said to me, "Oh my goodness, is Skip okay?"

I looked over my shoulder and saw Skip sitting on a bench. He looked terrible. His color was ashy, and he was sweating profusely. I walked over to him and asked, "Are you all right?"

"I feel kind of blah," Skip answered, "but I'll be okay."

When we arrived at Fenway Park, it got worse. Skip was completely disoriented. He couldn't remember how to get to the broadcast booth.

I'm not sure he even knew where he was.

I wanted him to go to the Braves clubhouse to be checked out by one of the team doctors, but Skip insisted that he would be fine if I just got him up to the booth. Against my better judgment, I did as he asked and got him up to the visitor's radio booth. Once there, he opened a medicine container and took a large, wafer-like tablet.

"Are you sure you're all right?" I asked.

"I will be," Skip said. "It's my diabetes acting up."

He seemed to be a little better by game time, but when the broadcast began, he kept calling the Red Sox the "Celtics," and during the first inning of the game, he actually fell asleep. I nudged Skip awake a couple of times. Eventually, he took another one of those oversized tablets and that seemed to do the trick. Within minutes, he had perked up and was more like his old self.

Skip had been diagnosed with diabetes in 1991, but this was the first time I had ever seen him have a work-related problem with it.

In fact, I always marveled at Skip's resilience as his health problems increased. Shortly after this episode in Boston, he had an angioplasty to clear a clogged artery. He received a pacemaker to control an irregular heartbeat in 2003, and he was hospitalized again in February 2004 with a variety of problems.

But after each episode, Skip would return with the same sharp wit and play-by-play talent as before. He had to change his lifestyle and watch his diet a little more, but he never lost that zest for having fun.

In 2005, the Braves offered the two of us an opportunity to have our own concession stand at Turner Field. "Skip and Pete's Hall of Fame Barbecue" became a fixture on the fan plaza. Each night, one of us would go out and sign autographs for 30 minutes or so. Skip would remind me from time to time to check out the food at our stand.

"You'll have to do it," he'd say. "I'm not supposed to eat any of that stuff. I'll have to wait for 'Skip and Pete's Hall of Fame Salad Bar.'"

In 2007, Skip decided to cut back on his travel. When the Braves hit the road that year, he would accompany us to the Eastern and Central time zones. But when the team went out West, he would take the time off and stay home.

Even this seemed to be wearing him down. On a late-August trip to Cincinnati, St. Louis, and Florida, he had some days when he really seemed to be out of sync. Something must have been going on. He told me about a month later that he remembered almost nothing about making that particular trip.

Shortly after the 2007 season ended, Skip was hospitalized with congestive heart failure. He almost didn't make it out. At one point, he slipped into a coma. But as his doctor, Charlie Wickliffe, later described, "The last time I was in his room one day, he was in a coma. The next time I went in, he was sitting on the side of the bed telling a joke. It was amazing."

Skip eventually went home, but for the first time in his Braves career, he was unable to go to spring training in 2008. He reduced his schedule even further, working only home games once the regular season began. His condition varied from game to game. Some days, he was his old self. Some days, he was obviously not feeling well. On a couple of occasions, he missed games because of his failing health.

Through all this, Skip was somehow able to maintain his great sense of humor and his unique broadcast style. There may have been nights when his delivery was a little slower and the speech a little slurry. But on most nights, you would never know anything was wrong with him.

He was one strong individual, and he loved his work.

In late July 2008, the Braves played a three-game series with the St. Louis Cardinals at Turner Field. In the final game of the series, on Thursday, July 31, Skip had one of his best broadcasts of the year. He was sharp, alert, quick, funny, opinionated, and more like the old Skip than he had been in quite awhile. I remember commenting after the game to our producer Jake Cook, "That's as good as he has sounded in a long time." Jake agreed.

Thus, it was surprising when Skip didn't come to work the next day for the opener of a three-game series with Milwaukee. His son, Chip, told us, "He's having a tough day. He hopes to be back tomorrow."

During the game, Skip even called our producer and told him he planned on being there tomorrow. But when Saturday arrived, Skip was still feeling lousy and didn't come in. He also didn't make it on Sunday. Joe Simpson called him that morning and reported that Skip just wasn't feeling very good.

The Braves won the final game of that Milwaukee series, 5–0. We then headed to the airport to board our Delta charter to San Francisco, where a series with the Giants would open the next night. It didn't seem unusual not having Skip on board. He hadn't made any of the West Coast trips in two years.

The seating arrangement on a team charter never varied. Bobby Cox and his coaches occupied first class. Just past the bulkhead is where the trainers, media relations personnel, and the broadcast crew were seated. The players were scattered throughout the rest of the plane.

Most of the time, the plane was big enough so that we each had our own row.

I was in my usual seat, six or seven rows back from the first class section, next to the window. At some point after we had departed Atlanta, I dozed off. I was awakened by a tap on my left shoulder.

When I opened my eyes and looked over, it was Bobby Cox sitting in the aisle seat. This was highly unusual. Bobby rarely came back to our portion of the plane, and if he did, he never sat down in one of the rows.

"Are you awake?" he asked.

"Yeah," I answered. "What's up?"

With a pained expression on his face, Bobby's words were blunt and direct.

"Skip passed away," he said.

"What?" I responded. "Oh no! What happened?"

"We're not sure," Bobby said. "Brad [Hainje, the Braves PR director] got an email. We don't even know how it got through; you're not supposed to be able to receive emails way up here. All we know is that it happened at his home sometime this afternoon. I wanted to personally give you this news. I'm awfully sorry."

"Wow," I said. I felt empty.

Bobby patted me on the shoulder as he got up to return to his seat in first class. Joe Simpson, who always sat directly behind me, leaned over my seat and asked, "Did I hear that correctly? Did Skip die?"

"Yeah, Joe," I answered. "That's what Bobby told me. I can't believe it."

As word began to circulate toward the back of the plane, players began coming to our seating area, asking, "Is it true what we're hearing?"

To all of them we had to say, "I'm afraid it is."

It was a sad and solemn group that landed in San Francisco and boarded the team buses for the long ride to the St. Francis Hotel. Once there, and after gathering our bags and getting them to our rooms, a group of us decided to walk across the street to Lefty O'Doul's, one of Skip's favorite watering holes.

The TV monitors at Lefty's were all tuned to ESPN and periodically, it would scroll across the bottom of the screen: "Longtime Braves Broadcaster Skip Caray Dies at 68."

It all seemed so unreal.

At some point, reliever Will Ohman asked, "What was Skip's drink?"

"Double Dewars on the rocks," I replied.

"Maybe we should all have one," Will suggested, but we declined. None of us were scotch drinkers.

"Well, let's order one for Skip," said Roger McDowell, our pitching coach.

That drink sat there the remainder of the night in front of an empty stool. Will, Roger, Joe Simpson, Jake Cook, and I, occasionally joined by others, reminisced about our fallen partner.

Lefty's was crowded that night. Whenever someone would approach that empty stool and ask, "Is anyone sitting here?" Roger would quickly answer, "Yes, that seat is taken."

The rest of that road trip is kind of a blur. The days were spent mostly making or answering phone calls or responding to emails. We learned more details about Skip's passing. He had collapsed while filling a bird feeder in his back yard. "What happened," Dr. Wickliffe said, "was Skip's great, generous, wonderful heart just gave out."

In the evenings, the games went on. Mark Lemke, one of our radio pregame and postgame hosts, flew out to work the games with me in place of Chip, who was back in Atlanta helping with the funeral arrangements.

After three games in San Francisco and four in Arizona, we returned home. The scheduled off day—Monday, August 11—was now the day for our sad farewell to our friend and partner.

An overflow crowd packed the Cathedral of Christ the King. I had been asked by Skip's family to deliver one of the eulogies. Normally, I was very comfortable in front of any microphone, but on this day, it was very difficult.

My tribute focused on the fun Skip and I had during the more than 5,000 games we had worked together, and how we found something to laugh about every day. I concluded with these words:

"I know all of you are here today to say goodbye to Skip. But Skip hasn't gone anywhere. He is going to be with us forever. Every day we'll hear that voice. Every day we'll remember that wit, that humor.

"Every day we'll recall that attitude. So instead of saying goodbye, I'm just going to say thank you. Thank you, Skip, for letting all of us be a part of your life."

Among the eulogists that day was Jiggs McDonald, former broadcaster for the Atlanta Flames and Skip's longtime friend. Jiggs, I thought, summed up Skip's life perfectly when he said, "Everybody dies, but not everybody lives. My friend Skip lived." Never were truer words spoken.

The following morning, a second memorial service, open to the public, was held at Turner Field. Georgia Governor Sonny Perdue was among those paying tribute to one of Atlanta's and Georgia's most recognizable icons.

The rest of the season went on, but with very little meaning. The Braves were well out of the NL East race and went on to lose 90 games, the club's most since 1990. And Skip's death had created a great void, not only on the broadcasts but all around the press box, where Skip was often found telling his latest joke or stirring up a little mischief.

About a month after Skip's funeral, I received a call from TBS Executive Producer Jeff Behnke, inviting me to be one of the play-by-play announcers for the network's 2008 postseason coverage. I turned him down. Even if I hadn't been contemplating retirement, my answer would have been the same.

TBS hadn't been very supportive of either Skip or me for the past six years. They had bumped us from the telecasts in 2003, bumped us again when the team was sold in 2007 and hadn't used either one of us for their initial year of playoff coverage at the end of the 2007 season.

I'll be damned if I was going to let the death of my friend and longtime partner create a bridge to win me back.

As the season wound down, my decision to retire became firm. I would give the team the two weeks after the season to think about it, as they had requested. But I could see nothing that would change my mind.

I had a great career, far exceeding anything I had ever hoped to accomplish. I wanted to leave on my own terms while I was still young enough and healthy enough to enjoy my retirement. The time was right.

On Sunday, September 28, at approximately 4:25 PM EST, Brian McCann fouled out to Houston third baseman Jose Castillo. That ended the Braves' 2008 season with a 3–1 loss to the Astros at Minute Maid Park. With the call of that play, my 43-year career in broadcasting came to an end.

Chapter **19**

So You Want to be a Big League Broadcaster

There is one thing you learn very quickly when you enter the field of broadcasting sports. You can't please everybody. One size does not fit all.

There are as many different styles of sportscasting as there are sportscasters. In baseball, you have classic storytellers like Vin Scully of the Dodgers, who paint vivid word pictures. You have iconic legends such as Ernie Harwell of Detroit, Jack Buck of St. Louis, or Marty Brennaman of Cincinnati, whose friendly voices become a hallmark for their team. There are bigger-than-life entertainers (Harry Caray, Dizzy Dean), home team rooters (Ken "Hawk" Harrelson, Mike Shannon), unforgettable voices (Mel Allen, Harry Kalas), guys with a gimmick (John "A-bomb for A-Rod" Sterling, Chris "Place Nickname Here" Berman), and steady professionals (Bob Costas, Dave Van Horne).

All have had successful careers with a style that is completely their own. But all of them share three traits that make up the foundation of the profession. I call them the three "C's"—credibility, commitment, and the ability to communicate.

Credibility may be the most important of the three. No matter how much you think you know about the game, there is somebody out there listening or watching who knows more. If you are going to tell a story about Willie Mays, you'd better get it right, because Willie may be watching. Got an interesting stat? Make sure it's accurate, because some listener out there is sitting at a computer screen looking at that precise information. Credibility issues have probably ended more careers in sports broadcasting than any other factor.

Commitment to the game and the profession is mandatory. For eight months out of every year, you are going to be spending more time with the team and your broadcast partners than you are with your family.

You are going to be traveling extensively, working irregular hours (sometimes in inclement weather), and missing a lot of family moments. One phrase you'll hear often is, "Dad can't make it, he has a game." It can be a glamorous and very rewarding life, but there are sacrifices involved. You and your family have to be willing to make them.

The ability to communicate is an obvious essential. That's what we are paid to do—communicate with listeners and viewers. Any former major league player has credibility. They played the game. But I've known some who, despite their commitment, have failed as broadcasters because they just couldn't put their thoughts and experiences into concise, meaningful words.

You often hear stories of people in baseball, both on and off the field, and their passion for the game. I can't think of a single group that demonstrates that passion more than the fraternity of broadcasters.

Almost every one of us has wanted to do this kind of work since we were little kids. We can't wait to get to the ballpark every day to see what's going to happen, what kind of stories are going to unfold.

We love the game's history, tradition, rhythm, drama, unpredictability, and excitement. And we revel in our good fortune to be able to be part of it each and every day.

We even love the mundane work that comes before every broadcast—the preparation. I can't ever remember arriving at Dodgers Stadium when Vin Scully wasn't already there, working on his notes for the upcoming game. Whenever the Philadelphia Phillies came to Atlanta, Harry Kalas was always at the ballpark, putting together his notes long before the team arrived.

That preparation includes interaction with players and managers.

Whenever we played the Cardinals or the Reds, you would always see Jack Buck or Marty Brennaman making the rounds down on the field during batting practice. The great ones don't become great by accident.

The two most well-prepared broadcasters that I ever worked with were in two different sports: Hubie Brown in basketball, and Dave Campbell in baseball. Whenever I worked an NBA game with Hubie or a Baseball Network game with Dave, they would arrive with a set of voluminous notes. So many notes, in fact, that there was no possible way they could use all of them in one game. But they had every conceivable situation covered, and nothing could come up in a game that they weren't ready to address with the appropriate facts and figures.

It is this preparation combined with passion for the game that leads to the high level of performance that good broadcasters consistently give.

Once the game starts, I always felt that a broadcaster had three responsibilities. Call them the three "E's"—educate, entertain, and enjoy.

As a broadcaster, you are privy to a lot of information that the average fan doesn't have. When pertinent, pass it along. Maybe it's something a player told you, maybe it's some fact or trend you uncovered during your preparation, but it all adds up to a better broadcast.

Good analysts are good educators. Don Sutton is excellent at taking you inside a pitcher's mind or analyzing his mechanics. I was always learning something new from Don, which was why I enjoyed working with him so much.

There is a knack to passing along this education or any information that is delivered during a broadcast. Think of the teachers you had during your school years. Who do you remember most? Those who delivered a dull lecture, or those who did so in an entertaining way?

Easy choice, isn't it?

Skip Caray had a simple philosophy of broadcasting: "Tell the truth…have some fun." And that was pretty much how we approached each and every game. We always tried to be honest, and we always remembered to laugh.

We frequently heard this comment from fans:

"You guys seem to be having so much fun on the broadcasts."

Well, that's because we were. We enjoyed being together. While we took our jobs seriously, we didn't take ourselves that way. We weren't afraid of a little self-directed humor. We had a good time each and every day.

There weren't many broadcast teams quite like ours. The closest thing to it then and now would be the Philadelphia Phillies group. Whether it was the old blend of Harry Kalas, Richie Ashburn, Chris Wheeler, and Andy Musser, or today's combination of Wheeler, Scott Franzke, Larry Andersen, Tom McCarthy, and Gary Matthews, it's a good, solid broadcast, and the broadcasters are having fun.

Of course, no matter how good you think you are, there are people out there listening and watching who can't stand you. Even at the height of our popularity, we had our critics. The most common complaints:

"Pete is too bland.... Ernie's an old fuddy-duddy.... Skip's a pompous cynic.... Don's too full of himself.... Joe's too vanilla." Those kinds of reviews come with the territory. Fortunately, we didn't have too many of them.

Baseball broadcasting is also a very provincial calling. You are always going to be most admired by fans of your team. Every region of the country thinks that their local broadcasters are the best. And that's the way it should be. It means that the broadcasters are doing their job. The Superstation gave us national exposure, so we developed fans everywhere—but only because they became Braves fans. Our province was a little larger.

Today's technology allows you to watch or listen to games from every team at any time. I've been doing a lot of that since I retired.

Without naming names, here are some of the things that I like and don't like about the current baseball broadcast scene.

On television, I like all of the additional camera angles now available. They provide us with a second or even a third look at any play that's close. In most cases, they clearly show whether the right or wrong call was made.

But I'm getting a little concerned about all of the clutter on the screen. That little box with the score, the count, etc. (called the "bug") is fine. But how many more station or network logos, pitch boxes, scrolling scoreboards, etc., will be put on the screen before we'll hardly be able to see the game?

Also, I know the bills have to be paid, but I wish there was a better way to do it. Producers have a laundry list of sponsor drop-ins that they have to get in during every broadcast. Some of these may have nothing to do with what's currently going on in the game, but if the drop-in is scheduled for the bottom half of the eighth inning, that's where it has to go. It might be the defensive play of the game that happened back in the third inning, but producers have to force it in even if it interrupts what may be the decisive moment of the game.

Wouldn't it be better if these sponsor mentions came at the beginning of the inning so that play could proceed uninterrupted?

In addition, do we really need a cartoonish animation and sound effect before every replay?

Here's something you should know. Most of the bells and whistles that are added to televised sports are not there because the fans demand it. They are there because TV producers can do it. If a team or network develops a new gimmick, it's almost immediately copied by everyone, as if to say, "See, we can do that, too."

Here's something you can try. Every now and then, ESPN Classic shows a baseball broadcast from the 1950s or '60s. Watch one of these games when you get a chance. There aren't as many camera angles and the graphics are primitive, but if you're a baseball fan, I'll bet you won't enjoy the game any less because there's not a *whoosh!* sound before they show you who's warming up in the bullpen.

I've got some beefs on the radio side, too. Attention all radio broadcasters! Don't forget to give the score! Broadcasting legend Red Barber used to use an egg timer to remind himself to give the score at least once every three minutes. I always tried to remember to give the score at least once during every hitter's at bat. Sometimes I'd forget, but it was a habit I tried to develop. There is nothing more frustrating than getting in your car, turning on a game and having an entire half-inning go by before you find out the score. That should never happen.

Also, there is a difference between radio and television play-by-play.

On radio, you have to describe the action. On television, you are putting captions on pictures. There is a difference. If you are listening to a game on radio, you should be able to visualize what is taking place. Good radio broadcasters paint the picture very well.

"Ground ball to short…Smith fields and throws…in time," tells me a little.

"Two-hopper to short…Smith, a step to his right, makes the back-handed pick-up…throws to first…got him by two steps" tells me much more.

Some of the young broadcasters who have been raised on television don't seem to understand this difference.

There are also ways to describe plays in an entertaining fashion. The great Ernie Harwell once turned a routine call into a classic line.

Detroit shortstop Eddie Brinkman committed an error, and Ernie's description said it all: "He played every hop perfectly except for that last one." I was in my car driving home from work in Toledo when I heard this line. I remember thinking at the time, "*Brilliant.*"

I also believe that we have to be very careful not to overwhelm the listener or viewer with numbers. This may sound like heresy coming from me, since I was known as a stats-oriented broadcaster, but I pretty much stuck to the basics and tried to use the numbers judiciously.

Today, there's an information overload in baseball. So many new stats and permutations of old ones are now available, and there are fans out there that want to hear them. But the majority have little comprehension of a hitter's OPS (on-base percentage plus slugging percentage) or a pitcher's WHIP (walks + hits per innings pitched).

There's a delicate balance that has to be struck in a broadcast. I've always believed you should keep a broadcast simple enough for the casual fan to understand with just enough material to satisfy the more sophisticated follower of the game. The fan that wants everything broken down into situational sub-categories is probably sitting in front of a computer screen doing this himself. He (or she) may care what Chipper Jones is hitting after the seventh inning with runners in scoring position and less than two outs, but most fans couldn't care less.

You can make statistics say anything you want them to. Today's printouts have every hitter's performance broken down inning by inning. If a hitter is 5-for-10 in the seventh inning, 5-for-10 in the eighth inning, and 0-for-10 in the ninth inning, what are you going to say when he comes to bat in the ninth? That he's hitting .333 after the seventh inning or .000 in the ninth inning? And does it really matter? The hitter you want up there is the guy hitting .333 for the year, regardless of the inning.

The other thing that numbers need is some perspective. Greg Maddux having a 1.56 earned-run average in 1994 is very impressive. Having that ERA in a year when the National League ERA was 4.22 is mind-boggling.

Some of the stats that are around today strike me as bogus. Take the so-called "quality start." A pitcher gets credit for a quality start if he pitches at least six innings and gives up no more than three runs. If a pitcher met the minimum requirements (6 innings pitched, three runs allowed) in every start and all those runs were earned, he would finish the season with an ERA of 4.50. In the expansion era (since 1961), the league ERA has been as high as 4.50 in the American League just 10 times and in the National League only twice.

That means that in most years you are, at times, rewarding a pitcher with a quality start when he has turned in a performance worse than the league average. That definition needs to be changed. If there has to be such a thing as a "quality start," it should require at least 6 innings giving up no more than two runs or 7 innings giving up no more than three.

Baseball is a game where statistics measure everything. They are important. But as broadcasters, we shouldn't overuse them. Whenever Skip was asked what he thought the most important statistic was, he would quickly answer, "Wins."

There's never been a better time to be a baseball broadcaster than now. Satellite and computer technology have made it possible for all games, on both radio and TV, to be heard and seen everywhere. Every broadcast is now its own version of what TBS was back in the '80s and '90s.

Research and game preparation have never been easier, thanks to the Internet. But the basics for those behind the microphone, I believe, are the same:

"Educate…Entertain…Enjoy." Or as Skip put it, "Tell the truth…have some fun."

There are a lot of good, young broadcasters who are beginning to make their mark in the business. I hope all of them have as long and successful a career as I did.

Chapter **20**

Reflections on a Fortunate Life

O n April 10, 2009, the Braves honored me at Turner Field prior to their home opener with the Washington Nationals. There were generous gifts, a video tribute, and the christening of the radio booth as the "Pete Van Wieren Broadcast Booth." The TV booth had been named for Skip in 2008.

I was truly touched by these gestures and appreciated greatly the warm reception given to me by the sellout crowd. I was also somewhat nervous. After the ceremonies were over, they had asked me to throw out the first pitch. If you've ever had a chance to do something like this, you know what I mean. The last thing you want to do is go out to that mound and make a fool of yourself in front of 50,000 people. You want that delivery to make it all the way to home plate.

You don't want to bounce it.

I had been playing catch with my son, Steve, in his backyard for the past three days. First, I had to make sure I could still throw the ball 60' 6". Then it was a matter of just loosening up the old arm and trying to keep it loose. Even with that preparation, when they handed me the ball and directed me out to the mound, I could feel my heart pounding.

Braves utility man Greg Norton came out to catch the ceremonial pitch.

He looked like he was 100 feet away, and when he squatted and presented the target, that glove looked about the size of a dime. When the pitch made it all the way into the glove (it may have even been a strike), I felt like I had just struck out the side.

When I arrived back in the Braves dugout, Bobby Cox came over, patted me on the back and said, "Nice pitch." Good ol' Bobby. He's always been a player's manager.

I made it back to the ballpark a few more times in 2009, and each time, Bobby would ask me about being retired. How was it? Was I finding enough things to do? How badly did I miss being around the game every day? As it turns out, he was more than just curious. Late in the season, Bobby announced that 2010 would be his final year as Braves manager. He, too, is retiring.

So is George Grande, the Cincinnati Reds television announcer, one of the many broadcasters who called me after I stepped down. So is Chuck Dowdle, a longtime Atlanta TV sports anchor. Looks like I might have started something.

There's one thing I can tell them all. Even though you are letting go of the game, the game will never let go of you. I find myself watching as much baseball as I did when I was working, maybe even more. I still follow the game as closely as ever, and I can't see that ever changing.

The game has been my life, and when you retire, you have plenty of time to reflect on what a wonderful life it has been.

You start out wanting to play. I remember as a kid paying my 25 cents to join the Rochester Red Wings Knot-Hole Gang. With that membership card, you could get into any Saturday home game for a dime. I never missed those Saturday games, and I would sit high up in the grandstand with all the other Knot-Hole Gang members, dreaming of the day when I would be down on that field playing.

When I got a little older, I would ride my bicycle to Red Wing Stadium. You could park it in a bike rack back then, and it would still be there after the game. I would try to get there early when the players were still arriving. I'll never forget the day Bobby Del Greco, an outfielder for the Montreal Royals and future major leaguer, saw me standing there and said, "Hey kid, come on." As we walked through the player's entrance, Del Greco told the security guard, "He's with me." He took me into the clubhouse, then out onto the field where several of the early arriving Royals players were taking some extra batting practice. Then he tossed me a glove.

"Go on out there and shag," he said.

For the next half hour or so, I was in my glory, running down balls in the Red Wing Stadium outfield.

When it becomes evident that playing for a living is not an option, you set your sights on other facets of the game. For me it was the broadcast booth or the press box—anything that would keep me close to the game. To have been able to go out and actually realize that dream was truly a blessing.

All those years in minor league markets made me appreciate it even more when that major league offer came. Then I wound up working for someone like Ted Turner and became part of his ingenious endeavors.

I'm often asked what it was like working for Ted. While I always mention the excitement and tremendous fun we had, I always remember to add that Ted was one of the most honest, loyal, and trustworthy people with whom I've ever been associated. Was it crazy at times? Sure. Were there days when I felt overwhelmed by the workload? Absolutely.

Would I do it all again? In a heartbeat.

When you reflect on a long broadcast career, you tend to dwell on those special moments, so many of which I have related in this book.

But you also have to chuckle at some of the gaffes that occurred.

During a game with the Cincinnati Reds in the mid-1970s, Braves catcher Vic Correll hit a high pop foul over near the seats alongside the first base dugout. Johnny Bench flipped off his mask, raced over, leaned over the railing, and made the catch for the third out of the inning. Working on the radio side, I totaled up the inning and sent it to a commercial break. When I looked back down on the field, Correll was stepping back into the batter's box. Bench had not caught the ball, or if he had, he had dropped it. Correll was still batting. Vic grounded out to end the inning, but our listeners never heard it. They were hearing a commercial.

When we got back from the break, I did the only thing you can do in such a situation. After wiping the egg from my face, I explained what had happened, apologized, and moved on. That is the only solution when you make a mistake on the air. And we all make them. You have to admit your error and correct it. If you don't, listeners or viewers may think that you are unaware you screwed up. And that creates credibility issues.

As embarrassing as that was, it didn't come close to the classic goof that occurred when Skip and Ernie were working the television side during a game against the Phillies. Mike Schmidt had just hit a home run. During the replay, Skip tried to say, "Boy, that Schmidt sure is strong!" But he left out a letter.

What the viewers heard was, "Boy, that shit sure is strong!"

Nothing was said for a moment as the next hitter stepped in. Ernie called the next couple of pitches, each followed by a pregnant pause.

Finally, he could hold back no longer, and to Skip he said, "What was that Phillies player's name again?"

The two erupted in laughter, and viewers who wondered if they had heard correctly now knew that they had. Humor had defused the whole situation. Again, when a mistake happens, get it out in the open and admit it. We're all human.

One thing I've been able to appreciate more and more as I look back on my career is the amazing 14-year run of division titles that the Braves put together from 1991 to 2005. Even in retrospect, that seems like an impossible achievement. It takes so much to win just one division title. If you can do it in back-to-back years, you've really accomplished something. But 14 straight is fairytale stuff.

Fans who started following the Braves in 1991 at the age of 8 or 9 were married with children of their own before they ever experienced an October postseason when the Braves weren't playing.

I am outraged whenever I see the Braves of that era referred to as the "Buffalo Bills of baseball." That reference is occasionally made because of the Braves' failure to win more than just the one World Series title. Certainly, a few more championships would have been welcome.

If Lonnie Smith hadn't hesitated on the base paths in 1991...if Mark Wohlers had thrown Jim Leyritz a fastball instead of a slider in 1996...maybe there would have been a couple more championships. But you can't take away winning that 162-game regular-season grind 14 straight times. The day I start believing that it isn't a remarkable achievement will be the day somebody else does it.

I know this much—it turned around the image of Atlanta as a baseball town. In 1976, my first year in Atlanta, the Braves drew 818,000 fans. In 1993, they had drawn that many by mid-May and finished the season with a total attendance just less than 3.9 million. It was a remarkable thing to witness.

When Atlanta started the string of titles in 1991, word leaked out that there were tickets available for the NLCS games the Braves would play in Pittsburgh. They were quickly grabbed up by Braves fans. Planes were chartered in Atlanta to fly the fans up to Pittsburgh on the day of the game. Buses took them to Three Rivers Stadium. After cheering for the Braves from their nosebleed seats, they headed back to the airport and flew back to Atlanta that same night. Now that is what I call support.

* * *

It wasn't all champagne and roses. There are some things I truly regret. For instance, I wish we had done a better job with the whole steroid situation. I think everybody connected with baseball during that time feels the same way. It's hard to put into words exactly how this whole problem escalated to the level that it did.

Did we suspect something unusual was going on? Yes, we did. And by we, I mean everyone from the commissioner on down—general managers, managers, coaches, trainers, broadcasters, writers. Everyone. It wasn't hard to see.

Some players were showing up incredibly bigger and stronger than they had been the year before. Home runs were being hit at a record pace, and they were being hit distances we never thought possible. This wasn't happening because everyone was eating their spinach. Something else was contributing to this. And we all had a pretty good idea of what it was.

But it was almost like baseball had a "Don't ask, don't tell" policy in effect. There was a lot of private speculation over who was and wasn't on the "juice." But you dared not make an accusation. No one that I know ever directly asked a player if he was using anything, and it was certainly not information a player would volunteer.

Whatever was going on was occurring surreptitiously. All we had were innuendo and rumors. When the cover finally blew, I think all of us were stunned by how widespread the use of performance-enhancing drugs was and which players were involved.

We should have started asking questions sooner. But so should have team executives, managers, team doctors, and others. We all share part of the blame.

As for the records that were set during this era, they have to stand.

There is nothing that can be done about that. For the fact of the matter is this: Even though we know much more now than we did while all of this was going on, we have little if any proof of anything.

Only a handful of players have fessed up. I doubt many will.

Every fan, every writer with a Hall of Fame ballot, and every future historian will have to make their own judgment call on this. Barry Bonds…Roger Clemens…Mark McGwire…Sammy Sosa…Hall of Famers or not? Bonds and Clemens, at least, were headed that way before their names were linked to this issue. Whether it is a permanent or temporary roadblock remains to be seen.

If you are familiar with my broadcasting style, you know how enamored I am with baseball history and records. One of the things that made game preparation so enjoyable for me is my love of research. I truly enjoy digging through old box scores, newspaper stories, record books, and magazines, hoping to hit on some interesting fact I never knew before. Whenever I could, I would share those findings with viewers and listeners.

One area I never paid much attention to until recently is my own vocation, broadcasting. Since I'm no longer on the air, this book is the only way I can tell you what I found.

There have certainly been major league broadcasters with longer careers than my 33 years, but not all that many spent the entire time with the same team. One who has is Vin Scully of the Los Angeles Dodgers. Vin has been broadcasting Dodgers baseball since 1950 when the team was still in Brooklyn.

The 2009 season was Scully's 60th year as a Dodger broadcaster. Now there's a baseball record that will never be broken.

But what about broadcast teams? For the purpose of this survey, I had to define "broadcast team" loosely. There has been so much movement back and forth between radio and TV, mixing and matching with other partners, that it's almost impossible to determine who was in one booth or the other at any given time. But it's not beyond the realm of research to link a pair of broadcasters to one franchise for a span of years. So that is how I proceeded.

At the top of the list—the Dodgers again. Jaime Jarrin joined the team as the Spanish play-by-play announcer in 1959 and is still going strong. So he and Vin Scully have been together as multi-lingual Dodgers voices for 51 years.

Second in longevity—the New York Mets duo of Bob Murphy and Ralph Kiner. Those two and Lindsey Nelson were the original Mets broadcast team in 1962. Nelson moved to the San Francisco Giants after the 1978 season. But Murphy and Kiner were part of the Mets broadcast package for 42 years. Murphy retired after the 2003 season. Kiner still makes occasional appearances on Mets telecasts.

The third-longest stretch goes to Ernie Harwell and George Kell of the Detroit Tigers. The two worked together only part of the time. Harwell was most often the radio voice, while Kell worked exclusively on the TV side. Tigers fans enjoyed the work of these two fine broadcasters for 36 of the 37-year stretch between 1960 and 1996. The lone exception was 1992, when Harwell was let go by the Tigers new ownership. The fans outcry brought him back in 1993. Sound familiar?

Kell retired after the 1996 season. Harwell continued as a Tiger voice through the 2002 campaign.

Number four on the list—the Cincinnati Reds twosome of Marty Brennaman and Joe Nuxhall. These two probably hold the record for the most games actually worked together. They were the Reds' radio team from 1974 through 2007, although Nuxhall worked a reduced schedule after the 2004 season. Still, "Marty and Joe" had a 34-year run.

Marty, of course, still is the voice of the Reds.

And in fifth place, I'm proud to say, is the team of Skip Caray and Pete Van Wieren.

We started together in 1976 and when Skip died, we were finishing up our 33rd year together. As a lover of baseball history, I am honored to be in such hallowed company.

Of course, you don't think about these kinds of things while you're working. At least, I didn't. Don Sutton said to me one day, "Some people want to be good at what they do, some want to be known for what they do. You're in that first group."

He's right about that. I never sought the spotlight. All I ever tried to do was to go to the ballpark every day and deliver the best broadcast I could. I never had that "perfect" broadcast. I always felt there was something I could have said or done a little better. But I'm proud of my body of work. I tried to give my best effort every day.

When I was working in Binghamton back in the late 1960s, I had to fill in for our morning radio show host, Jack Murphy, while he went on a two-week vacation. I was quite nervous about this assignment. "Murph" had the highest-rated radio program in the market, and I didn't want to screw it up. Before he left, I asked him if he had any advice for me.

"Just talk to one person," he said. "That's what radio is—just you and the listener."

That maxim stayed with me my entire career. Whenever I was on the air, I knew there may be a million people listening. But I tried to talk to them as if they were one person. I've received a lot of accolades since retiring. But the one that meant the most to me was that single line from Furman Bisher's *Atlanta Journal-Constitution* column on October 25, 2008:

"He makes me feel that I'm right there beside him and he's talking right in my ear."

I was, Furman. I was. To you and every other single listener out there. I could not have asked for a better validation of what I tried to do in my career than those words from Furman.

There is a lie that every baseball broadcaster tells anytime he is asked the question, "Who do you work for?" The answer given is always the name of a team, a station, or a network. But we're all wrong. We work for you—the viewer, the listener, the fan. Without your support, we don't get very far.

So to all of you who ever tuned in to a Braves game on radio or television and enjoyed our work, thank you. We couldn't have done it without you.

To all of you who lobbied so hard to get Skip and me back on TBS in 2003, thank you. I can't tell you how much that support meant to both of us during that difficult time.

To all of you who worked on the management side with the Braves and our radio affiliates, and to most of the management team at TBS, thank you. Thank you for giving me the opportunity to live out my dream on such a big stage.

To all of the Braves' players, coaches, and managers, especially Bobby Cox, thank you for providing so many thrilling moments down on the field. It was a privilege to serve as your broadcaster.

To all of you who worked alongside me in the broadcast booth, thank you. I never knew going to work every day could be so much fun, and you guys are the reason.

To all of you who worked behind the scenes on the telecasts and radio broadcasts, thank you. It was a pleasure to work with each and every one of you.

To all the members of the press corps, thank you for your many years of friendship and for all the kind words you wrote about our broadcasts.

And finally, to all the members of the Van Wieren family—Elaine, Mom, Jon, Angel, Steve, Starla, Chaney, Grace, and Rebecca—thank you. It's been a pretty amazing ride. I couldn't have taken it without your love and support.

If nothing else, after my father's transgressions, I hope I have restored respectability to the Van Wieren family name.

Acknowledgments

First of all, I would like to thank my coauthor, Jack Wilkinson. His encouragement kept me going, his suggestions prompted memories, and his sharp eye kept this from being a book full of dots and dashes.

My wife of 45 years, Elaine, kept clippings, programs, and other mementos of just about everything that happened in our lives. These proved invaluable in checking details and exact quotes. Her management of our finances and everything connected with our home also allowed me to fully pursue my career. I certainly chose the right girl.

The Atlanta Braves came through whenever needed. Special thanks to Beth Marshall, the team's director of public relations.

Manuel's Tavern provided Jack and me with a place to meet. In fact, they gave us an entire wing of their establishment to spread out and work undisturbed. Thank you Brian Maloof, Bill McCloskey, Pat Glass, Bobby Agee, Curtis McBride, Erin Schopf, Jeremy Aggers, Laura Krueger, Steve Pitts, Laura Winters, Charlie Moseley, Michelle English, Ian Hills, Stanley Barnes, Scott Jerine, Susan Strack, Adam Lowe, and David Maloof for your kindness and hospitality.

Whenever game details became a little fuzzy, I could always rely on Baseball-Reference.com or Retrosheet.org to clarify things. Thanks to the creators of two of the best websites on the planet.

And finally, thanks to Mitch Rogatz, Tom Bast, Adam Motin, and Karen O'Brien of Triumph Books for giving me the opportunity to tell my story.

—Pete Van Wieren

The only thing better than listening to Pete call a game is doing his book with him. A pleasure, Professor, and a privilege. For Janet, as always, and for Ali and Katharine. My sister Kathleen and the Stanton men, our long-distance tech guys: John, Kyle and Ian. The hacks: Steve Hummer, Bill Rankin, and Tom Stinson. The Doc: fellow escapee Paul Shea. *Click:* Patty Rasmussen and Pouya Dianat. Thanks to Paula Caray and Chip Caray. Of course, to Mitch Rogatz, Adam Motin, Karen O'Brien, and all the good folks at Triumph.

And in memory of Tom Wilkinson, Skip Caray and Paul Hemphill.

—Jack Wilkinson

Index

DISCARD

B VANWIEREN

Van Wieren, Pete.
Of mikes and men

METRO

R4001248774

METROPOLITAN
Atlanta-Fulton Public Library